The Reality Sutras

Seeking the Heart of Trika Shaivism

Jaya Kula Press
110 Marginal Way, #196
Portland, Maine 04101
jayakula.org

© 2018 by Shambhavi Sarasvati

All rights reserved. No part of this book may be reproduced in any form, or by any means, without permission in writing from the publisher.

Cover and interior design and layout: Saskia Nicol
saskianicol.com

Library of Congress Control Number: 2018904586

Sarasvati, Shambhavi
The Reality Sutras: Seeking the Heart of Trika Shaivism

ISBN:
978-1-7322183-0-7 (pbk)   978-1-7322183-1-4 (ebk)

Printed in the United States of America on acid-free paper.

The Reality Sutras

Seeking the Heart of Trika Shaivism

Shambhavi Sarasvati

Jaya Kula Press Books

by Shambhavi Sarasvati

Pilgrims to Openness: Direct Realization Tantra in Everyday Life, 2009

The Play of Awakening: Adventures on the Path of Direct Realization Tantra, 2012

Returning: Exhortations, Advice and Encouragement from the Heart of Direct Realization Practice, 2015

No Retreat: Poems on the Way to Waking Up, 2016

Nine Poisons, Nine Medicines, Nine Fruits, 2017

The Reality Sutras: Seeking the Heart of Trika Shaivism, 2018

My wish is to be neither an ascetic
Indifferent to the world
Nor a manipulator of supernatural powers
Nor even a worshiper craving liberation—
But only to become drunk
On the abundant wine of devotion.

—Utpaladeva, Shaiva Devotional Songs of Kashmir[1]

As far as the space of the universe extends, so far extends the space within the heart. Within it are contained both heaven and earth, both fire and air, both sun and moon, lightning and the stars.

—The Chandogya Upanishad[2]

CONTENTS

Two Handfuls of Rice 13

1 Reality is knowable 16
2 Everything is God 18
3 Your senses are for directly discovering your real nature 20
4 God is wisdom virtue 22
5 Desire is required 25
6 Freedom is the unlimited capacity for self-expression 28
7 Shakti is the power of self-reflection 31
8 All self-reflections are enjoyed by the Lord 33
9 Diversity is a real experience 35
10 Know yourself and know God 38
11 There are no individuals 41
12 Worlds are experiences 44
13 Belief, faith, and trust are obstacles to self-realization 49
14 I am here, I am everywhere 51
15 Unmind the mind 54
16 There is no emptiness 57
17 Impermanence is the glamour of God 60
18 The whole of life is the means of realizing the Self 63
19 God is both the limited and the unlimited 66
20 Ignorance of your real nature is the cause of suffering 70

21	There is no suffering	73
22	Manifest life is a cascade of becoming and unbecoming	77
23	Maya makes diversity for the Lord	80
24	All is perfection	82
25	Recognize, gain confidence, and immerse yourself in presence	85
26	Guru is the View, the method, and the fruit	88
27	Lose the watcher	92
28	The mind is the organ of curiosity	94
29	The relative purpose of life is self-realization	96
30	Duality is for the enjoyment of reciprocity	99
31	Rest in your real nature	102
32	Ananda is aesthetic appreciation	105
33	Everything is equality	107
34	Ethics are already built in	110
35	The heart is the gateway to unconditioned wisdom	114
36	Devotion is wisdom's crucible	116
37	The View expires	118

Keep on Continuing 120

*For disciples and devotees of **that***

Two Handfuls of Rice

I am writing this book as a small offering to my students and to all those who desire to better understand the View of Trika Shaivism, also known as Shaiva Tantra. Students of other direct realization traditions, such as Dzogchen and Chan Buddhism, will find much resonance here.

The Sanskrit word for View is *darshan*. In Tibetan, View is *tawa*. View has a few special meanings in direct realization traditions. It means both to see and what we see as a result of doing spiritual practice. It also means the instruments through which we see and a way of living that embodies the wisdom we directly encounter through spiritual practice.

View teachings let us know what our traditions have to say about existence, cosmology, the self, God, consciousness, and realization. In the direct realization traditions, we say: *Learn the View, practice with the View, embody the View.* When we have recognized our real nature and, through practice, come to embody the teachings in our perceptions and activities, we are said to be living the View.

Studying the View of your tradition is critical to practicing correctly. This is easy to understand. If I go for a walk in the woods, and my orientation is that I am trying to catch a glimpse of a certain rare bird, I may find that bird. If my orientation is that I am simply walking along and enjoying being outside, I will likely achieve that, but I probably will not find the bird.

Likewise, some people perform rituals with the View that they are propitiating great beings in order to accumulate merit. In direct realization traditions, we are more likely to perform ritual with the View that we are trying to recognize our own, already perfect wisdom nature through the medium of the ritual. To a great extent, the View with which you practice determines the result. For this reason, it is important to understand the View of any tradition in which you are participating so that you can practice correctly and move without undue delay toward realizing what that tradition has to offer.

View and the role of textual study

In direct realization traditions, the teacher, the teachings, and the practices you do all help you to directly recognize or encounter your primordially enlightened nature. You directly realize the nature of your self, of reality, through a process of opening the gates of the senses, including the mind.

The word in Sanskrit for direct realization is *pratyakshadarshana*. *Pratyaksha* means "direct." So pratyakshadarshana means directly experiencing or having the darshan of the ultimate nature of reality with your own senses. Direct realization is not primarily an intellectual understanding; it is 100% embodied, useable, experiential wisdom about how you and life actually are.

Despite popular and erroneous notions that direct realization traditions are all about effortless, "sudden enlightenment," both *sadhana* (spiritual practice) and textual study are emphasized. In combination with oral instruction and practice, studying the texts of a tradition helps us to clarify, enlarge, and guide our understanding of View.

Some students approach text study in a more intellectual way as if they were reading philosophy or theory. But for a student who is ripe, reading about the View can act as a potent catalyst for directly relaxing constricting patterns of body, energy, and mind. For this reason, students are advised to read and also to meditate on key teaching texts.

What kind of book is this?

The Reality Sutras is a handbook of View teachings. I am doing my best to make essential aspects of the View of my Indian tradition accessible to contemporary students. For the most part, I am reporting on what I have discovered for myself through engaging in spiritual practice. My hope is that *The Reality Sutras* will inform, but foremost that it will serve as a source of contemplative material for practitioners. Occasionally I enrich a passage with a quote from my root Guru, Anandamayi Ma. She was not a teacher of Trika Shaivism, but her teachings were always about directly realizing the nature of the Self.

You won't find many footnotes here. I am not making a conventional effort to convince you that I know what I'm talking about or that my tradition's View of reality is one you should adopt. More than proving something to your intellect, I would prefer to move you. From my perspective, the only desirable proof of my little offering is whatever response of "yes" you discover within yourself and then whatever unfolds after that.

With infinite love,
Shambhavi
Portland, Maine

1

Reality is knowable

The nature of reality, your own nature, is an open secret announcing itself everywhere and always available to be directly known and more fully embodied.

Many spiritual traditions hold the View that reality is unknowable or a mystery. This makes sense only if what you mean by "knowable" is "explainable." Of course, we cannot capture and explain every aspect of reality with words or even with numbers.

Let's say you take a workshop describing all of the different styles of meditation, their histories, and how people have practiced in different spiritual traditions. You even read some scientific studies about the effects of meditation. But after a long period of gathering descriptions, explanations, and information, you still do not have much understanding of meditation. In order to have real knowledge of meditation, you have to meditate!

Meditation and other spiritual practices require you to engage your body, your energy, and your mind. They are embodied, experiential, and immersive. Knowing in the direct realization spiritual traditions means that by doing spiritual practices such as meditation, you can directly discover the real nature of the Self and existence. Using your five senses and your mind, you can find out who and what you are and how things work.

The discovery of your real nature is not just information. It is embodied knowledge. By practicing just with your body, energy, and mind, you transform your moment-to-moment experience. You begin to have spontaneous insights into fundamental processes of reality. You enter into a rich conversation with our alive, aware world. You ultimately discover the capacity to interact directly with the subtlest aspects of nature, including space and time.

The knowledge, or more properly wisdom, one gains by doing consistent spiritual practice is instantly usable. It is much more thoroughgoing than an explanation, and yet it cannot be explained by ordinary means. It can be pointed toward, experientially revealed, and demonstrated. The goal of spiritual practice is not to comprehensively describe or neatly explain reality, or to dominate it, but to be able to respond to life with unrestrained compassion, clarity, intelligence, creativity, and spontaneity. Enlightened, embodied wisdom is always in action. Ultimately it is action that emerges from and expresses the wisdom of the heart.

We call that which we discover through sadhana by many names: God, Self, reality, Shiva Nature, nature of mind, Buddha Nature, Christ consciousness, Krishna consciousness, aware livingness, instant presence, flowing presence, essence nature, or the natural state. My Guru, Anandamayi Ma, simply called it *that*.

2

Everything is God

All worlds, all creatures, and existence itself are made of and full of a single, continuous, self-aware consciousness and its creative energy.

Consciousness and energy are the ground and the substance of your existence. Always together, with no experience of separation, they comprise an infinite ocean of unconditioned awareness and its creative potency. From this ocean, the experiences of the diverse forms of manifest life naturally arise like waves. The waves of manifest life are made by the ocean of consciousness and energy, arise within that ocean, dissolve back into that ocean, and are composed of that ocean.

The ocean and its waves are a living symbol. A living symbol is one that doesn't just represent what it symbolizes in an arbitrary way, but one that actually partakes of what it symbolizes or is an aspect or direct expression of what it symbolizes. When you do spiritual practice, living symbols can appear in your mind or in visions to teach you about how reality works. You will definitely start to notice that many important aspects of our world function as living symbols.

You may find it helpful to meditate on living symbols or observe them in your day-to-day life. For instance, gazing at the ocean and remembering the View can give you a direct experience of the nature of reality. The ocean and its waves are an important living symbol for direct realization practitioners.

When we first begin doing sadhana, we embody the erroneous conviction that we are individual waves moving along in space without an ocean. We feel fragile and separate. Our experience is characterized by loneliness, aggression, and defensiveness. As we progress in our practice, we begin to experience the reintegration of body, energy, and mind with that continuous ocean of living presence.

The Sanskrit word for reintegration or immersion is *samavesha*. Rather than intellectually understanding the natural state, or witnessing something, we are actually trying to rediscover our continuity with living presence. We are trying to discover that the ubiquitous ocean of living awareness is our real nature, not separate from or different from us. We practice to remain consciously immersed in that.

The base state of reality, living presence, may be too subtle for our ordinary senses to discover right now. But if our senses are a little more open, presence itself, the livingness of everything, will become definite and palpable. We learn directly for ourselves that this living presence is continuous, eternal, and uncaused. We learn through our senses and our mind that it sits behind all phenomena, giving rise to all from within itself.

3

Your senses are for directly discovering your real nature

Sadhana frees our limited senses to directly encounter their continuity with reality's infinite capacities for seeing, hearing, touching, tasting, and smelling and with infinite mind.

You may have noticed that some people's senses are sharper or duller than others. Listening to a complex piece of music, some people are going to hear more nuance and others less. Some people have a more vibrant experience of color or a more refined and subtle sense of taste. When our senses are dulled, we cannot participate or express ourselves fully. You can understand this from your ordinary experience. When you have a head cold, your senses are dulled, and you feel less able to engage with life. The clarity and openness of our senses affect our relationship to everything.

Now imagine that the senses, including mind, are notes on an infinite piano keyboard. The senses of most human beings fall along about two octaves, ranging from the dullest to the most keen of us. But there are infinite other notes representing refinements and expansions of the senses that most of us cannot even imagine in our current condition. Sadhana opens our senses so that we can play and enjoy more of the notes.

Sadhana works by eroding our experience of being separate individuals. Over a long time, our experience of our senses also becomes less individualized. Our taste, touch, hearing, seeing, smelling, and sensing with our mind literally escape the boundaries of individuality and become more continuous with the senses of the larger reality, a.k.a. God. Or you could say that the field of the play our senses becomes larger.

This release of the senses from the cage of individualism will enable you to explore the depths of life without a microscope and to see far flung times and places without a telescope or a time machine. You will gain understanding of how reality works directly from reality itself, and you will be able to participate and express yourself more fully.

But we should not get stuck here. The essence of self-realization is not to wield spiritual powers. The essence of self-realization is to embody cosmic wisdom virtues such as compassion, kindness, clarity, skillfulness in action, and mercy. You become established in the heart. For a person who has some actual realization, any special skillfulness of the senses that develops will naturally be used to shower virtue on everyone.

4

God is wisdom virtue

God is unconditioned, unrestrained, and spontaneous intelligence, compassion, mercy, generosity, creativity, curiosity, precision, patience, and clarity.

God has many names. In Trika Shaivism, God means all of reality, all of existence. God means *that* living awareness, *that* supreme subjectivity with no cause, no outside, and no other.

When I was first learning Tantrik sadhana, my teacher used words such as "omnipotent," "omniscient," and "omnipresent" to describe God. I did not find this inspiring. In fact, I found such descriptors to be clinical and abstract. I had entered the practice feeling that I did not believe in God. I wanted to know about reality. In my limited View, reality and God were different, and God did not seem necessary. So I put God on a back burner and just focused on my sadhana without much understanding of what "God" might refer to.

Years later, I encountered my Guru, Anandamayi Ma. She had already ceased to inhabit a human form, but as I learned, she was and is still very much here. Through a special experience, she taught me about the real nature of God.

One of Anandamayi Ma's main ashrams sits on the banks of the Ganga in Varanasi, just north of Assi Ghat. I had no experience with ashrams or temples and felt timid entering either. Upon crossing the threshold of the ashram, a young Bengali man greeted me. He was not a sannyasin, but was engaged in full-time seva as an administrative assistant and science teacher in the ashram school.

We chatted for some minutes. He served me chai. At some point, he said, "You should visit the balcony. Ma always gave satsang there. Westerners never visit it, but you should go there." He pointed toward an external stairway leading up to the second floor.

I walked up the stairs, admiring the panoramic view of the river. Reaching the top of the stairs, I discovered a spacious balcony and further on, the hall that bounded the ashram's living quarters.

When I took my first step onto the balcony, the sky seemed to open and from it poured a river of grace directly into the top of my head. I remember looking up and seeing nothing but an infinite expanse of dancing, golden-blue light.

I felt a force and a shock of understanding and surrender moving through me. I stumbled a few more steps onto the balcony and fell to my knees weeping. I experienced the entire sky entering me as a river made of endlessly flowing compassion.

For the next hour, an utterly palpable intelligence and compassion poured into me. I wept without restraint. I understood it was my Guru. I understood directly, incontrovertibly, that compassion is not something we "have" or "cultivate," but that it is woven into the fabric of reality itself. I understood that reality, Guru, and God are not different from that wisdom. I also understood that there is only benevolence.

When we are relatively ignorant of our real nature, our experience is more monodimensionally physical. Beings and things appear to our senses to be composed only of gross materials. When we are a little more awake, we can experience subtle energy. Later, if our perceptions become even more subtle, we can sense living presence: a pervasive awareness or consciousness and its vitality. But the ultimate insight into the nature of reality is that it is composed of wisdom.

Through this direct perception, we learn that God is primordial intelligence, compassion, mercy, generosity, creativity, curiosity, precision, patience, playfulness, and clarity. Consciousness and energy are one way of talking about this living awareness. But in the end, we discover that wisdom is the real name of God. We learn that the ocean of consciousness and energy is an ocean of awake, alive, creative, responsive wisdom: the Supreme Self.

5

Desire is required

The unstoppable desire to find out who you really are is the voice of the supreme wisdom speaking to you from within you.

You often hear that being spiritual requires getting rid of desire. Nothing could be further from the truth. We absolutely need desire in order to wake up. Desire is not only necessary, it is at the heart of reality, inciting the creation to unfurl from the unconditioned.

In the tradition of Trika Shaivism, Shiva is the personification of awareness. Shakti is the personification of creative potency or power. Impelling the creation is Shakti. She excites Shiva to endlessly overflow with the play of linear time, space, beings, and worlds. This objectless, self-expressive desire is the cosmic-sized version of our more limited desires.

Our desires are conditioned. We want this and not that. Shiva's desire is pure self-expression, pure self-enjoyment. God is not journeying toward wisdom; the Lord is wisdom. But we ourselves are *that* enacting the play of a return from ignorance to wisdom purely for fun. Desire directs our participation in the game of self-realization. But first, our desire must recalibrate. It must redirect from desperately desiring limited objects such as a donut, a car, a lover, a vacation, or spiritual powers, to desperately desiring to wake up.

Luckily for us, there is only one desire. The desire for a donut is not different from the desire for self-realization. Our simple cravings are "stepped down" expressions of the desire to wake up. There is only one Shakti (energy) of desire. She just expresses herself differently depending on conditioning. The myriad limited desires that drive you every moment of the day eventually merge into one great desire: the desire to discover who you really are. This is a natural, unavoidable process.

Desires for objects of desire, even self-realization, are based on a feeling of lack, or incompletion. When we discover the desire to self-realize, we begin to move toward embodying objectless desire and unconditioned, joyful self-expression.

The Sanskrit phrase for the Shakti or energy of desire is *iccha shakti*. This is often crudely translated as "will." In fact, translating iccha shakti as will creates misunderstanding. We can hardly fathom the objectless desire that is iccha shakti. We tend to interpret it in an ordinary way as the will of an individual to accomplish specific goals, or intentions.

A better translation of iccha shakti is "desire" or "inclination" or "impulse." A natural and objectless impulse for self-expression engenders endless effulgence: the mad overflowing we call manifest life. Iccha shakti is not separate from reality's pure enjoyment of its own plenitude.

You may be able to relate this to the experience of generosity. When you are feeling self-protective, fragile, or lacking, you will likely take some time making decisions about giving. You may worry about boundaries, about not having enough, or about some future possible calamity. You may deploy a semblance of generosity in order to gain admiration and feel more secure. You will be cautious about generosity or perhaps behave in a generous-looking way instead of just being generous.

If you are not worried about yourself, if you feel nourished by life, when the urge to be generous arises, you will be more likely to simply follow it. Feeling nourished and content are great forms of wealth. They cause you to overflow spontaneously with generous thoughts, feelings, and actions. When you feel replete, there is no resistance to generosity. It is a natural and joyful self-expression.

From the absolute perspective, all action is impelled by iccha shakti. All activity is generosity. On one level, all is generosity because something exists rather than nothing. On another level, all is generosity because there is nothing but beneficence. All activity is happening spontaneously and is nothing but self-expression: a celebration of the nature of existence.

Anandamayi Ma had her own way of talking about iccha shakti. She called it *kheyal*. Kheyal is a type of Indian improvisational vocal music. Ma said innumerable times that she never did anything unless moved to do so by kheyal. She meant that in her activities, she directly embodied the spontaneity, playfulness, and natural generosity of the creator. We are not quite "there" yet, but our effortful pursuit of self-realization will eventually lead to effortless, beneficent overflow.

6

Freedom is the unlimited capacity for self-expression

Svatantrya means the independent freedom to manifest unlimited and unconditioned experiences of form and circumstance.

When we consider freedom from our limited perspective, we may think of being able to do whatever we like or of being free from obstruction. The inherent freedom of reality includes the possibility of these freedoms, but it is more expansive. This alive, aware reality possesses total freedom of self-expression. This freedom is not dependent on any other entity, situation, or cause. In the Trika tradition, the primordial, independent freedom of reality to express itself is called *svatantrya*.

You and I share an experience of dependency. We are dependent on many circumstances and fundamentally on the natural, unconditioned state just as a wave is dependent on the ocean. Every choice we make—to eat, to sleep, to breathe, to travel, to take a particular job, to do or not do absolutely anything—is dependent on many other beings and circumstances. For starters, we are dependent on others for getting born!

Shiva Nature, on the other hand, is unborn and uncaused. It is the ground of existence. There is nothing prior to it or behind it.

We can better understand svatantrya if we consider the living symbol of a mirror. A mirror can reflect anything put in front of it. It has infinite potential for creating reflections. A mirror will also provide reflections regardless of the nature of the objects place in front of it. It is unconditioned by likes and dislikes or by any concept whatsoever.

Likewise, this ever-fresh, awake, and creative reality has infinite potential to spontaneously cause reflections, or appearings, of infinite forms and circumstances to arise within itself. But the mirror-like quality of reality is different from an ordinary mirror. There is no outside of the mirror of reality. Just as waves arise from ocean and are made of ocean, the reflections that arise in the mirror of consciousness are made of consciousness and its energy. They are reflections that arise in the mirror of consciousness without an object outside of the mirror to cause the reflection. The mirror is the cause of the reflection. The mirror is another living symbol, like the ocean, that is useful for direct realization practitioners.

Svatantrya, unlimited freedom of self-expression, also includes the capacity to create the appearance of limitation for the purpose of giving rise to different kinds of experiences. For instance, if you want to have metal utensils for eating, you must limit the potential of metal. Molten metal has the potential to be formed into many, many different objects. By specifically fashioning a fork or a spoon, you are limiting that potential. You have taken away, at least temporarily, the potential of the metal to be an earring or a nail. You would have to melt the fork down again into its molten, less conditioned state in order to again reveal its less conditioned capacity.

Svatantrya and the capacity for self-limiting are also mirrored in our own capacity for acting in a drama. In a play or a movie, you may act the part of a person with only one leg. You really have two legs, but it's fun and challenging to try to embody a one-legged person's experience.

    Similarly, a single subjectivity plays all of the roles in all of existence. Limitation is how the vast display of diversity is manifested out of the unlimited and unconditioned. However, there is not really any limitation. There is a play of limitation. Just as in the example of a two-legged person playing the part of a one-legged person, this alive, aware reality is always present in full measure and full capacity.

7

Shakti is the power of self-reflection

The primordial clear light of awareness and its power to self-reflect are the origin of dualistic experience.

Consciousness, or Shiva, appears to us as *prakasha*, the light of primordial awareness. Shakti, or *vimarsha*, is the primordial capacity to self-reflect. Pure awareness by itself would be totally passive. The power of self-reflection is the origin of all experience and of the totality of diverse appearings from the most limited to the most universal.

When we self-reflect in an ordinary way, we initiate an experience of the three poles of duality. I am the observer, a.k.a. the observing subject or the active subjectivity. That is one pole. Then there is the second pole: the act of observing. Finally, even when engaging in internal self-reflection, we are establishing an "object" of contemplation: ourselves. This is the third pole. These three poles of subject, act, and object constitute the architecture of all dualistic experiences of people, objects, and worlds.

When we self-reflect, we are enacting an experience of one

reflecting on itself as if there were two. For instance, when I self-reflect and observe that I am writing a book, there is an upsurge of something like an appearance of duality. In truth, the person observing, the act of observing, and the person writing are one and the same. Just because I can reflect on myself, I am not fooled into thinking I am multiple people! Yet, within myself, I am enacting a play of duality.

As we self-reflect, so does the ultimate. Beginning with the primordial capacity for self-reflection, Shakti wields the power to generate experiences of more than two. Beginning with self-awareness, the appearance of an external other is projected, seemingly outward, but actually still within the one subjectivity of the Supreme.

Together, awareness and its Shakti generate the infinite experiences we call duality or impermanence. But as we do, they never experience any separation even while they continuously express and contemplate the nature of Self through all experiences of people, beings, worlds, and circumstances.

8

All self-reflections are enjoyed by the Lord

Everything that appears is a reflection of the nature of one uncaused and continuous subjectivity in a state of self-contemplation and self-enjoyment.

In Trika Shaivism, the word "reflection" refers to any appearing of any form or circumstance. This alive, aware, naturally effulgent reality spontaneously gives rise to infinite self-expressions. These self-expressions constitute all manifest life. This pervasive living presence enjoys experiencing reflections of its own nature in the same way that we enjoy anything we have made as a reflection of who and what we are.

When we paint, or sculpt, or dance, or write, or compose music, we enjoy stepping back and contemplating what we have made. We have externalized a self-expression, but that object or experience continues to have an uncannily intimate relationship with its creator. The alchemy and magnetism of self-expression resides, in part, in the pleasurable confusion of outside and inside.

Likewise, all of reality ceaselessly emits the conditioned

experiences of form we call individuals, worlds, and circumstances. These are its own creations and reflections of its own nature. While there is no outside to that supreme subjectivity, the Supreme has the power to produce experiences of the diversity of worlds and experience them as if they were objective or external. It does this in order to contemplate and enjoy them, just as we do.

The nature of reality is to give rise to appearings which, on a relative level, do not enjoy the full awareness and potency of the whole. Although seemingly limited, all reflections announce in their arising the essence of their origin. Returning to the example of art created by human beings, in these productions, we can discover a lot about human nature. Just so, in the reflections, the appearings, of the creation, we can discover the nature of reality itself. Discovering that is the aim of sadhana.

Whether Shiva-Shakti is making a planet, a race of sentient beings, a tool, a tree, or a rock, through this process of self-limitation, there is enjoyment and the opportunity to reflect on its own nature. This divine enjoyment, or contemplation, is aesthetic self-appreciation on an unimaginable scale.

9

Diversity is a real experience

Existence encompasses both continuity and the experience of diversity. Neither is to be rejected.

Right now, you are likely experiencing the world as a collection of beings and objects with empty space separating them. This is duality, or *bheda*: the experience of separation, the experience of more than one.

When our day-to-day experience is that of being a separate individual, we are under the influence of *anavamala*. Anavamala is the root ignorance: the conviction that we are separate bodies, each with our own, separate consciousness. One way of talking about the goal of spiritual practice in Trika Shaivism is that it relieves you of anavamala.

Dualistic perception has three poles, or three reference points: the perceiver, the act of perceiving, and the perceived. Experiencing life from the vantage point of a separate perceiver engaged in an act of perception of other objects and beings is a habit. It is an engrained habit, but a habit nonetheless. This habit can be unlearned. The fact that it can be unlearned, or simply abandoned, strongly indicates that it may not be the bottom line for reality. Nonetheless, dualistic experience arises naturally as an aspect of the expressiveness of living presence.

Nondual experience, or *abheda*, arises when perceiver, the act of perception, and the seen are experienced as one continuous, undivided circumstance with no actual separation between the three poles. When you have the embodied, consistent perception that the ground is continuity, not separation, you are still enjoying the experience of the diversity of people and objects. In fact, you enjoy diversity more because you move from the earnestness of dualistic karmic vision to appreciating diversity as a playful display that does not in any way depart from continuity.

Some traditions, particularly orthodox Hindu and Buddhist traditions, teach that manifest life is unreal or illusory. The Views of these traditions range from extreme negations of the reality of manifest life, to positioning dualistic experience as a trick or a veil, to assertions that transitory phenomena are unreal simply because they are transitory.

Trika Shaivism teaches that, while there are not actually separate objects and beings, the experience of separation is real and natural. So is unlearning it. Once having unlearned the habit of separatist experience, of separatist awareness, we can enjoy the multiplicity as the ornament and creative glamour of God. This condition of enjoying manifest life while not experiencing separation is called *jivanmukti*, or liberated in life.

Continuity and the enjoyment of diversity co-exist and are both of the real nature of existence. This experience of wildly proliferating diversity, and particularly the experience of communicating, is the delight to be found in embodied life. When we relax and realize that separation is an experience emerging from within continuity, then suffering ends, and we can enjoy the carnival of diversity. An experience of tremendous intimacy arises that is a hallmark of self-realization.

In traditions that denigrate dualistic experience, or deny its validity, practices of withdrawal of the senses are more common. But in direct realization traditions, we are generally doing practices to release our senses from limitation, not cut them off. We are trying to reunite our senses with the more expansive sense capacities of reality as a whole and thus become more like Shiva.

> [It] is Siva Himself, of un-impeded Will and pellucid consciousness, who is ever sparkling in my heart. It is His highest Sakti Herself that is ever playing on the edge of my senses.
> — Abhinavagupta[3]

God is not focusing on one person's breath or withdrawing from sense experiences. God's "one-pointedness" is everywhere, all at once. Direct realization View leads one more in the direction of practices that are based on opening the gates of the senses, although there is no prescription against doing practices of limited one-pointedness if that would be helpful. We don't reject anything.

At some point, distinctions such as dual and nondual stop being important. There is only aware livingness forever accomplishing its own nature. One becomes immersed in the immediacy of that, and discussions of withdrawing or participating, of eyes closed or eyes open, of duality and nonduality become utterly irrelevant in the face of the unbroken fullness and majesty of life.

10

Know yourself and know God

What we have been seeking to know is our own, already enlightened essence nature. Recognizing the Self, we experience it everywhere.

When we wake up, we discover that the fundamental nature of all of reality is self-aware, creative subjectivity. We come to know this infinite subjectivity as our very own self and the self of all else. Whether we first experience this self as being "out there," or "inside" makes no difference. Eventually there is no inside and no outside. Recognizing essence nature anywhere enables you to recognize it everywhere. This is a core teaching of both Trika Shaivism and my root Guru, Anandamayi Ma.

One time, a student of mine began to practice *sahaja*, or non-conceptual, open-eyed contemplation. When you first begin to practice sahaja, it feels quite austere. But as you continue, it becomes the most relaxed and engaging practice in the world. In fact, sahaja means naturalness.

After my student had been doing the practice for a while, she reported feeling spooked because she was having the experience of someone sneaking up on her from behind. She was beginning to sense presence.

Presence is what we can call our experience of pervasive vitality and awareness. Going deeper into presence over time, we encounter wisdom itself. Instead of experiencing space as empty and objects as dead "stuff," we recognize and become immersed in the friendliness, liveliness, and intelligence of everything.

Many people writing about Tantra focus on experiences of energy. However, the ultimate fruit of practice is usable wisdom, not simple experiences of energy. This must be kept firmly in mind so that one does not get stuck.

The job of the teacher is to directly introduce students to living presence. This is called "transmission." Transmission is a natural circumstance through which the student experiences the essence state of the teacher, or the primordial Self, in themselves.

Some people think that transmission means the teacher is giving you energy, or giving you something you lack. Nothing could be further from the truth. It is a disservice to students to teach them this falsehood. You already have everything; you are perfect and complete. Transmission is an experiential reminder of who and what you already are. In fact, transmission only works because your essence nature and that of the teacher are the same and continuous.

The experience of lack, or incompletion, is an aspect of impermanence and, on one level, an expression of the cosmic Guru function. Because of our experience of lack, we also experience longing. It is longing that ultimately impels us to seek to know our real nature. But our real nature is eternal. What we discover in a transmission situation is the eternal, always and already indwelling in all.

Students who understand how to work in a direct realization tradition know that transmission gives you an experience of the fruit of the practice. Then you do your practice to discover the fruit in yourself. You can use transmission as a beacon. In Vajrayana traditions, this is called "taking the fruit for the path."

For instance, if you move to my neighborhood, I might drive you around and show you the locations of the grocery store, the parks, and cafes. But later, when I am not around, you have to find these places on your own. You have to remember the experience of driving to those locations and feel your way back to them. For the purpose of this analogy, I am assuming you are not using GPS!

Just so, recalling the feeling-sense of transmission, the student uses sadhana to find their way back to that. Sadhana is the method we use to walk back to our semi-forgotten primordial, enlightened nature.

The ancient Tantras teach that you do not have to go anywhere to find God, to find the Self. This living presence is everywhere, and is in fact the real nature of all phenomena. Everything you need to discover has already been given to you, right where you are, here, now, and always. All of the wisdom you might discover "out there" is alive in your body, your mind, and your very own breath. So instead of beginning at the beginning, you begin at the end. You begin with a taste of the awake state and continually call that forth to guide you home.

11

There are no individuals

Most people have the experience of being a distinct body surrounded by empty space. This is a real experience, but it is not your real condition.

Let's go back to the ocean and its waves. The ocean is a living symbol of the continuity of consciousness and energy. Out of the ocean, waves arise and subside. All of the beings, plants, and manifestations of this world are like those waves.

You can recognize a wave, but if you consider a wave more deeply, you realize that a wave has no life apart from the ocean. In fact, a wave is made by the ocean, made of the ocean and is continuous with the ocean. A wave is an aspect of the ocean, not separate from it. A wave is completely dependent on the ocean, and each wave is a product of the whole ocean. Importantly, you cannot specify where a wave ends and the rest of the ocean begins.

Just like waves, our bodies, emotions, and minds are infinite events of consciousness and energy. Our forms arise out of the ocean of consciousness and energy, are made of that ocean, and remain always continuous with it.

We are individual stylings, or style waves of God, but we are not separate from the whole. We are waves having experiences of being particles. We are one body with the capacity, the power, to produce experiences of multiplicity and distinction.

The natural condition of being a human style wave is that we forget to greater or lesser extents that we are continuous with all else. When we are relatively unenlightened, we suffer from our experience of separation. We have to remember or rediscover continuity using a kind of disciplined approach we call sadhana. When we wake up, we can understand that the experience of distinct form is a source of delight.

Our fear of and denial of impermanence also arises from the experience of separation. We have a fundamental understanding of the fragility of this form, and we generally try to defend ourselves. We defend our bodies, we defend our minds, and we defend our self-concept in our attempt to create a situation in which we can hide from impermanence and feel safe.

Imagine if a wave thought itself to have an independent existence. Instead of knowing itself to be a scion of a vast, powerful, magnificent, eternal, and shining ocean of life, it felt separate and vulnerable. The wave might try to defend its existence, just as we do. Swimming among a bunch of defensive, aggressive waves, each trying to maintain its own territory, would not make for a fun swimming experience!

When we do spiritual practice, our sense of distinct physical boundary begins to soften and become more porous. Our self-concept begins to feel very limited and constricting as we have more direct engagements with living presence. We work harder to relax our limitations and become capable of encountering life in a less conditioned way.

We will always be able to recognize and work with our individual style-wave of consciousness and energy. However, the more we are able to integrate our awareness and energy with *the* awareness and energy, the more continuity rather than separation will become the basis for our lived experience.

12

Worlds are experiences

We live in a subjective, not an objective world. All worlds and beings, and the experience of objectivity itself, arise within a subjectivity.

How many times have you heard, "This is just my experience, but..."? You may not realize it, but this statement is a product of centuries-long debates about View.

In the common understanding of orthodox Western science and philosophy, a table is a real object that exists objectively outside of any person's experience of the table. Your experience and my experience are considered to be filters through which objectivity is distorted. We each encounter a slightly different table because we are experiencing it through our subjective senses. But outside of these, a real table exists, or so the story goes.

The terms "subjectivity" and "objectivity" have specific meanings in philosophical and scientific traditions. Subjectivity generally indicates a subject, an individual, with the capacity to self-reflect and some agency. The View of most Western philosophical traditions is that subjectivity is a lens through which individuals perceive reality in their own unique ways. Objectivity is when circumstances are viewed as they really are, not 'distorted' by a perceiving subject.

Objectivity can be used very loosely, for instance to describe supposedly unbiased journalism. But in its stricter scientific and philosophical senses, objectivity is a kind of holy grail that refers to a circumstance in which we would be able to encounter the world undistorted by our perceptions. In Kantian philosophy this is called *das Ding an sich*, or the thing in itself.

The glorification of objectivity comes at the expense of the denigration of experience. When we say, "this is just my experience," we are signaling our understanding that subjective perception does not accurately represent the objective real. In fact, we are saying that something outside of our experience always trumps experience.

This View has trained many people into believing that a so-called rational thought process also trumps modes of knowing via more immediate, sensory experience. I have noticed, among my students and other people, a degradation in their ability to access and trust the immediate wisdom that appears as a surge of inner knowing, or a prompting from our alive, aware world. These forms of experience are always available to us, but many of us have turned away from them.

In the Trika tradition, "objective" has a different meaning than it does in orthodox Western philosophy. Here, "objective" indicates that which has been emitted by and within the subjectivity. Objects and an objective world *experientially appear* to be external to that subjectivity. In other words, objective here means the appearing of an other, actually many others, from and within the body of the one. Subjectivity, or consciousness, is the foundation of all that is. Objectivity is a concept and an experiential mode being created by an omnipresent subjectivity.

Orthodox cultures of scientific rationalism have distrusted direct, sensory experience and have elevated the objective in status, even when the objective is considered to be unreachable for now. The discovery of more realized spiritual practitioners is that what we call matter is actually an experience made available by a subjectivity for itself. Shiva Nature's life process is to create experiences of external worlds and beings for its own enjoyment and then to discover through the play of awakening that they are not external at all.

More importantly, Trika practitioners come to understand that we live in a totally communicative and alive situation. No action goes unresponded to by the whole. Things and beings appear and resolve back to the unconditioned just like in an orchestra where instruments play and fall silent in response to each other and the guiding desire of the composer. Responsiveness, not objective material processes, are the basis of existence.

Returning to our table, these days we can say with scientific certainty that a table, or any other object, is mostly empty space populated by a combination of atoms and molecules. But how does this circumstance present us with experiential qualities such as form, hardness, smoothness, coolness, heaviness, and so on? Fairly recently, scientists have posited that "solid tableness" is produced as a result of human interaction with the states of energy that give the table texture and other qualities. This description of matter gets closer to what yogis in Tantrik traditions could have told scientists a thousand years ago. But there are significant differences between even this update and the experience of yogis.

For a Tantrik practitioner, or any practitioner with some realization, a chair is not "just" an experience with the objective chair hovering sadly out of reach. Nor is it fundamentally a combination of atoms and molecules interacting with an environment, although this would be a fine relative description of a chair. Consciousness and its energy, or wisdom, is the fundamental nature of matter, not atoms and molecules.

What we call "matter" are the appearings of Shiva Nature. It is Shiva Nature that is producing experiences of solidity out of itself.

The real nature of matter is a flow of responsive experience within a continuous subjectivity. Furthermore, a practitioner with some accomplishment can see, without any technological support other than years of sadhana, that a table is comprised of alive awareness and is continuous with all else. How is this so?

First it is necessary to understand that our physical eyes are not the organs of sight. They only serve as living symbols of the pervasive seeing power of this reality. In fact, all of our senses are the senses of all of reality showing up in a limited configuration as us. When we profoundly relax our body, energy, and mind, more subtle sight becomes available to us. We begin to participate in the expanded seeing that is happening everywhere. This is really not so hard to understand.

Even among ordinary people, there is a vast range of capacity to sense and see. Listening to music, some people will be able to hear with more precision and clarity. Relating to others, some people are able to more sensitively see and feel the condition of other people. Then there are people who have prescient dreams, or can effect subtle healings, or who can communicate to non-human beings.

When we consider this "ordinary" range of human senses, it is not so hard to understand that our senses have a lot more potential! If you have ever studied a spiritual tradition, or spent time with spiritual practitioners, you likely know that people with honest spiritual accomplishment have the most refined and expanded senses. They can galvanize people with their enormous compassion, insight, energy, and kindness. They can sometimes see the pasts and futures of others, even beyond this lifetime, walk through walls, produce objects out of "thin air," appear in two places at the same time, and similar activities. These occurrences are the result of the relaxation of one's self-concept and the resulting increasing integration of individual senses with the sense capacities of reality itself.

So, back to the table! When an accomplished practitioner looks at a table, they might see an ordinary table, but in some circumstances, they also might see a lively, variegated field of intelligent light that is continuous with and responsive to all else. The primordial intelligence of this light is communicated directly by itself. Just as we know a human being possesses intelligence by looking at them and engaging with them, we also recognize that intelligence and aliveness in everything when we perceive and engage with our more awake senses. We discover directly that this primordial consciousness is producing the experience of table out of its own body of awareness and energy and that "table" is continuous with the totality of the creation.

So in the Tantrik View, there is no objective chair "out there" beyond the reach of consciousness. Experience is primary. The chair, or any object, is an experience being produced by primordial consciousness and energy for its own enjoyment. The phenomenal world actually is a theater of experiences.

Our experience of waking up is the central drama in this theater. In order to play well, we must consult our own experience and learn to read the ways in which wisdom is communicating to us through our gross and subtle experiences. We must learn to follow and take refuge in the multi-faceted speaking of wisdom through every aspect of this theater of experience created by wisdom, for wisdom.

13

Belief, faith, and trust are obstacles to self-realization

We are explorers and experimenters. Our aim is to discover for ourselves the nature of reality and the Self.

Religions ask for your belief, faith, and trust. These foundations of religious doctrine and institutions don't require you to arrive at a more personal, direct, and incontrovertible experience. You can, if you like, rely on what you have read, or have been taught by an authority figure, or have been told to believe. This is, of course, very comforting for many people.

Trika Shaivism asks for your courage, your doubt, your persistence, your intelligence, your devotion, and your unstoppable desire to find out for yourself. The practices of Trika Shaivism and other direct realization traditions lead to concrete, practical, usable wisdom. They lead us to pass through doubt to unshakable confidence in the natural state.

In his commentary on the *Bhagavad Gita*, the great 10th century Kashmiri Tantrika Abhinavagupta writes: "The best candidate for instruction is a person who has doubts about the topic that is going to be presented."[4] Doubt is viewed as a soft, open position from which spiritual exploration becomes most possible and fruitful.

Hakuin Ekaku, a Zen teacher who lived at the cusp of the 17th and 18th centuries famously said: "At the bottom of great doubt lies great awakening. If you doubt fully, you will awaken fully."[5] The lesson is: Don't be afraid of doubt. Use it to get rid of everything other than what proves, through experience, to be incontrovertible.

Trika Shaivism is deeply devotional, but it is not a religion. It is more of a spiritual technology for clearing doubts about the nature of reality and becoming more spontaneous, skillful, expressive, and compassionate. You will be asked to test and experientially discover the View. You must be willing to do the work to find out for yourself using your body, energy, and mind. Your teacher will not be satisfied, or even pleased, with proclamations of trust and belief.

Pratyaksha pramanam means the exploratory, experimental process of "measuring" reality via the direct experience of the senses. It is understood that, along with some expert guidance, the human body, energy, and mind are your best tools for walking out of karmic obfuscations into the clarity of self-knowledge. Exploring step-by-step new landscapes of understanding; diving deep into the infinite subtleties of the heart; becoming fluent in the myriad languages of body, energy, and mind; discovering directly for yourself: this is the adventurous and uncompromising way of Trika.

14

I am here, I am everywhere

We are not in the business of destroying I-sense; we are in the business of liberating it from constraint.

If you hang out much around the spiritual water cooler, you hear talk about "getting rid of 'I'" or "getting rid of ego." Sometimes you can develop the idea that you are supposed to be floating around in a pink cloud of referenceless oneness. Some traditions hold this View, but in direct realization traditions, we are not trying to get rid of "I"; we are trying to free it from karmic conditioning.

A fundamental principle of reality is that it is simple and unified. Particular expressions of reality achieve diversity through processes of contraction and expansion. For instance, let's say I am a person who is always giving time and energy to my friends even when they don't want me to. I give because I desperately want people to be generous to me. I am trying to manipulate people into feeling that they need me and owe me.

I could also be someone who wants the world to be a better place to live. I give my time and energy to working for nonprofit organizations. But I have a very strong attachment to achieving specific outcomes with my giving. When circumstances don't go my way, I become angry and upset.

Finally, I could be a person who enjoys giving and who also has the clarity to be able to give skillfully. I understand that the outcomes of my giving are not up to me. I am just one factor, but I happily give anyway.

Each of these scenarios invokes the cosmic wisdom virtue of generosity. In the first scenario, "generosity" is under a lot of tension. The wisdom of generosity is shining through a dirty window we call karmic conditioning. The analogy that is used in the tradition is of the sun. The sun is always shining at full strength, but if there are clouds in the way, or dirt on the window, then the pattern of light changes, and the strength of the light is diminished.

Karma is patterns of consciousness and energy moving with momentum through time. The way that wisdom virtues show up in particular circumstances is shaped or colored by karma, until we are realized, that is. But the wisdom virtues are still shining like the sun.

In the second scenario, there is less obscuring karmic vision. This person is looking outward, and their field of concern is larger than the first person's. The pattern of karmic vision allows in a little more light. But generosity is still operating under tension.

The third situation is good, healthy, ordinary generosity. Wisdom is not too constricted or obscured.

Reality works the same way all the way through. There is no fundamental difference between expanded and contracted, heaven and earth, or wise and ignorant. Apparent differences are manifested along a continuum via varying degrees of limitation.

How do we apply this principle to I-sense, or self-awareness? Reality itself is self-aware; I-sense is pervasive. A famous Sanskrit mantra expresses this: *Aham.* The mantra means "I am." Aham is the cosmic "I am" that is being announced throughout every nook and cranny of manifest life.

Our gnarly, selfish, self-protective ego is that cosmic Aham under karmic tension. The same "I" principle, or self-awareness, operates at every level of life, but sometimes it is unable to fully express itself because of karmic obscurations. Insentience manifests when Aham is totally obscured, as in, for example, a toaster.

Our job as practitioners is to do sadhana and relax our karmic tensions. This process allows wisdom virtues to express more fully in and as us. Sadhana is actually a subtractive process. We are not cultivating wisdom, or transforming consciousness. Wisdom is already perfect and fully present. We are just cleaning the window, or blowing away the clouds. Then the small, cloudy self gladly rediscovers its identity with the sunlit I AM of all of creation.

15

Unmind the mind

That which arises, these appearings, come and go ceaselessly, and so the accomplished person remains undisturbed.

Spiritual traditions from various parts of the world place a great value on leaving behind impermanence and ascending to a heaven where everything supposedly remains unchanged for all eternity. In orthodox Hindu and Buddhist traditions, this emphasis sometimes finds expression in the valorization of other kinds of cessation of movement. There may be an emphasis on heroic feats such as stopping one's thoughts or one's breath; controlling the emission of sexual fluids; or externally remaining in a frozen, insensible, "spiritual" condition. People are admonished to close off, control, and chastise the senses. This View can also manifest as the desire to designate and then achieve a final spiritual accomplishment such as immortality or a light body.

Practitioners of Trika Shaivism hold the View that creating displays of phenomenal worlds is the natural life process of God.

Producing endless experiences of diversity is what God does, and this production never ceases entirely. Essence nature, the eternal, remains unaffected by the comings and goings of impermanence just as a mirror is unaffected by the reflections that appear in it. Yet the natural state of existence is not frozen. The alive quality of the base state could be described as a dynamic stillness.

Within the various Tantrik traditions, diversity and the continuous production of experiences of diversity are celebrated. And since God continually accomplishes its own nature everywhere, there is no place to escape to where the display of impermanence ceases. For a practitioner in a direct realization tradition, there is nothing to do but to discover how to remain undistracted, resting in one's own nature, while all of this apparent activity continues.

Wherever you go, to this world or some other, whatever body you inhabit, that of a human, an angel, or a siddha, you will still be in the midst of life. More importantly, since God is delighting in the creation, so must we as we wake up. Self-realization means being free of conditioning *and* enjoying the display of impermanence. My Dzogchen teacher Namkhai Norbu Rinpoche often summarizes the path and its fruit by saying: "We realize and we enjoy." The 14th century Maharastrian poet Jñanadeva expresses this beautifully.

> *The yoga that is attained by the yogis through the means like restraining the senses is as lustreless before this path as the moon is by day. There is no action or inaction, and everything goes on as the experience of the Atman. The non-dual one enters of his own accord the courtyard of duality. And the unity deepens along with the growth of difference.*[6]

Why restrain the senses when they are God's gateways for experiencing? Why leave duality when one can deepen the experience of unity here and also enjoy the astounding display of difference, of the multiplicity?

A common notion is that spiritual practice requires strict control of or monitoring of the mind. In the direct realization traditions, it is taught that one must "unmind the mind." Just as thorough realization means remaining undistracted by life's comings and goings, so we must also remain undistracted by what is happening in our minds.

Thoughts are patterned energy. The treasury of karmas stored in the mind is deep and fathomless. We may succeed in quieting our minds, or even experience periods of the cessation of gross thoughts. But so what? Untold *vritti*, or mind patterns, remain bubbling just below the surface. No one can control the mind in all circumstances, or for very long, or much at all if we account for the subtle vritti and not just gross thoughts. Sadhana does unwind karmic conditioning, including conditioned thought patterns, but it can never rid us of thoughts. Mind continues to do what mind does.

Realization means the ability to rest in your own nature in all circumstances, even unpleasant or difficult or busy circumstances. There is always a wiggle, always some disturbance in the world that might distract us. The only refuge is to discover living presence and integrate with that rather than running distractedly after what comes and goes, including the mind.

Thoughts arise, enjoy a life cycle, and then subside. Traffic continues to jam the roads. Neighbors argue. Children fall ill. Accidents are sudden. Storms rage. Wars erupt. Planets and entire universes blink in and out of existence. The question is not how can we get rid of disturbances, but how will we live at peace with it all.

16

There is no emptiness

Emptiness is an experience that serves as a gateway to recognizing the fullness of presence.

Emptiness may be one of the most misunderstood spiritual teachings of all time. This is not the fault of students. Teachers often misunderstand teachings about emptiness, or they have only received relative teachings on emptiness. Even when teachers do have a thorough understanding, they often hold back on mentioning that emptiness is a relative teaching, not a fundamental of the base state.

One time I was attending a Dzogchen teaching. The teacher whispered under his breath, "There is no such thing as emptiness." I waited eagerly for him to continue. I thought that finally the secret would be dragged out into the open! But he just continued teaching about emptiness in an ordinary, relative way.

When you do consistent spiritual practice, your limited concepts of body, energy, mind, and world begin to fall away. *Shunya*, or the experience of emptiness, is ushered in by the shock of recognizing that your ideas about life are not so incontrovertible, reliable, or solid as you had previously assumed. This introduces you to the experience of a void. You start to have experiences of free fall, of no ground. This is the real nature of the famed emptiness.

Shunya can also be like falling out of love. Everything feels flat and dull and pointless because you are no longer filling yourself with inflated ideas and emotions. You just can't get so worked up about yourself or the world anymore. But eventually you begin to perceive the more subtle beauty and possibilities in your new, less secure, less overwrought situation.

A student once announced her discovery that she has no soul. She was quite excited about this! Previous to studying in our tradition, she had cultivated the idea that inside of her fleshly body was something like a spiritual mini-me. This made her feel full and safe and important.

When she did enough practice, she discovered that body is not different from "spirit" and that even solid objects, such as her body, are more subtle than she had imagined. So she experienced a kind of relative emptiness.

Emptiness, or shunya, can take many forms. It can feel scary or exhilarating or both. The experience is definitely destabilizing. The bottom line is the recognition that manifestations of essence are provisional and ephemeral in substance and duration. These phenomena include our self-concepts, our beliefs, our cherished habits, our bodies, other beings, and worlds. We begin to feel and understand that the people, things, ideas, and circumstances we cling to so earnestly and deem to be so incredibly important are players in a fleeting, improvisational dance. As the famous Buddhist saying goes: "The bad news is you are falling. The good news is, there is no ground."

Weirdly, emptiness can be like a drug. One can get attached to the experience of emptiness, particularly if it is valorized by your teachers and traditions. The feeling of relative spaciousness can be quite pleasurable.

People can also become stuck in a kind of negative, grieving relationship to emptiness, especially if the experience is still somewhat conceptual, and you have not let go entirely. If you have what is called hungry ghost karmic vision, you have a habit of being attached to feelings of loss. So you may get mired in a kind of mournful relationship to the idea of shunya.

Concepts of emptiness can also become weapons brandished in a kind of gleefully bitter way. This is a form of spiritual bypassing. You wag the admonishing finger of emptiness when you think you perceive people being too attached to their concepts and habits. This creates a paradoxical situation in which you have made emptiness your new secure ground in a competitive sort of way.

In the best circumstance, shunya is a recalibration. Your entire sensorium has to become accustomed to a new perceptual situation. After what may be an initial period of feelings of destabilization and loss, shunya can usher in a refreshing lightness of being and willingness to explore and play with reality in a less earnest way.

In some traditions, the experience of emptiness, or shunya, is considered to be the final realization. Sutrayana Buddhist traditions hold that emptiness *is* the base state. This is their experience based on their practice. This is not true, however, for the practices of Trika Shaivism, Vajrayana, or Dzogchen. For direct realization traditions, the experience of shunya is only half-way there.

If you manage to deeply let go, if you look deeply into emptiness with your body, energy, and mind, what you discover is the fullness of living presence. *Purna Brahma Narayani* is a Sanskrit phrase that expresses the real nature of the base state: full of wisdom and creative energy. Passing through the gateway of shunya, you discover that there is not a single speck of emptiness anywhere.

17

Impermanence is the glamour of God

From the perspective of the realized self, the experience of impermanence is fundamentally enjoyable.

Impermanence is the experience of things coming and going. Some spiritual traditions deem impermanent manifestations, such as bodies and earthly life, to be degraded, lower, or lesser than in comparison to what does not come and go. Ephemerality is often spoken of in mournful tones and equated with suffering and being tricked.

If we think about it for a minute, there is nothing that necessarily links impermanence with degradation. Impermanence is just a natural fact of manifest life. Only a kind of religious-cultural bias links impermanence, bodies, and earthly life with unreality or degradation.

In the Abrahamic traditions, the fall of Adam and Eve into impermanence ushers in the state of sinfulness among humankind. In some Buddhist traditions, impermanence is equated with suffering or is charged with creating suffering simply by dint of being transitory.

In the View of Trika, Shakti continually excites Shiva to overflow with the creation. Shiva-Shakti produces the manifest out of the pure joy of self-expression. Manifest life is sometimes referred to in orgasmic terms as the "emission." There is no sense of degradation or sinfulness. Manifest life is a celebration of the nature of the Ultimate. Our job is to remember that and end our ignorance. Ignorance of the real nature of things is suffering, not sin.

While the experience of suffering is real, and we have to deal with it, we are already enjoying impermanence. To the extent that we are able to appreciate impermanence, we are being more like the awake Self.

We enjoy the turning of the leaves in fall. We enjoy yearning for an absent loved one. We enjoy watching our children and ourselves change over time. The feeling of loss itself can have a strong component of enjoyment. The short and fragile lives of butterflies fill us with wonder.

We also appreciate violent destruction. We love to watch buildings being demolished. We're fascinated by storms. When bombings, tsunamis, earthquakes, and volcanoes occur, we feel a mixture of fascination, awe, exhilaration, fright, and sadness. Our entire movie and gaming industries are largely built on our enjoyment of and fascination with destruction.

Some cultures have deeper understandings of our real relationship to impermanence. Japanese artisans create ceramic bowls and vases with cracks that are lovingly filled with gold. The cracks remind us of the impermanence of all objects. The gold draws our attention to the beauty of impermanence and our poignant attempts to thwart it.

The culture of Chinese Daoism encourages the cultivation and enjoyment of nostalgia: a gentle yet not unpainful mourning of missed opportunities, things past, and people who are out of reach. Many poems, paintings, and musical compositions from the Chinese Daoist tradition celebrate nostalgia. Nostalgia, in this context, is a vehicle for contemplating impermanence and enjoying it.

The root of generosity is that something is here rather than nothing. From the perspective of Trika Shaivism, the continual upsurge of infinite, impermanent manifestations is an expression of the generosity of God. In the Trika tradition, impermanent life is referred to as the "ornament" or "glamour" of God. Glamour is an ancient word for magic and magical spells as well as for beautiful adornment.

> *This Being is called Lord Śiva. He is the essence and existence of all beings. The external objective world is the expansion of His Power and it is filled with the glamour of the glory of God Consciousness.*
> — Abhinavagupta [7]

One time, years ago, my Buddhist roommate was doing her preliminary practices (*ngondro*). She had to make something like 300,000 offerings of the Vajra Guru mantra and rice. Along with the rice, she mixed in some sparkly coins and gems. Every few weeks after making her daily offerings, she had collected a large bowl of offered rice out of which were emerging the half-buried, colorful, shining objects.

I thought that my roommate's bowl of offerings was a perfect symbol of our circumstance. The rice was unconditioned Shiva Nature. The gems and coins partially emerging from that were our glamorous, diverse worlds. The whole was a single continuity.

Impermanence is not something we are trying to escape; it is made of God. Impermanence is God overflowing with the bliss of self-expression. When we stop suffering, we can remain and enjoy everything. We can be more like Shiva.

18

The whole of life is the means of realizing the Self

Everything here is a reflection of essence nature, and so we use our ordinary experience to walk backward out of conditioning and realize the Self.

Immanent to every aspect of impermanence is the eternal. No realization is complete without recognizing this. Realization means coming to know the alive, aware ground of existence, the continuity of wisdom virtue, as your own self. This continuity gives rise to all temporary phenomena, including your own individualized experience of body, energy, and mind. Recognizing impermanence is only half-way.

The Mother, Shakti, is the creatrix. The Father, Shiva, is the light of consciousness infusing all from within. The Mother and the Father are never apart. And so you cannot expect to find the ground of your existence, your real nature, anywhere but here in the midst of life. There is no outside.

Dualistic and transcendental spiritual traditions hold the View that there is an unbridgeable divide between matter and spirit and between sentient beings and God. The possibility of both sin and evil arises from this division. Matter, including bodies, appetites, and women, is degraded. Spirit is pure.

Direct realization traditions in general have no concept of sin or of salvation for that matter. If everything is made of and by enlightened essence nature, then sin cannot exist, and salvation is irrelevant. We are all already made of God from the beginning. We don't need to be saved.[7]

Our understanding of behaviors such as anger, jealousy, sadness, comfort-seeking, and greed is that they are the result of natural, Self-imposed limitations on the full flower of wisdom. Our limitations contain hidden seeds of wisdom virtue, and so wisdom may be discovered even in the midst of limitation. This means that no matter what condition you find yourself in, you can always discover the wisdom speaking to you in every situation. You can choose to follow that. Following wisdom is the royal road.

Everything we do, no matter how heinous, is an attempt to rediscover continuity. When a person forms or joins a cult, or some kind of segregated movement, they are trying to find connection. When a person drinks or does drugs, they are trying to relieve themselves of the boundaries and burdens of the small self. When a person harms themselves or others physically, they are still trying to experience some kind of continuity. A punch in the face is still a connection, albeit a very limited connection. Everyone in every circumstance is attempting to heal the experience of separation that we call anavamala.

In addition, because reality is simple, reiterating the same principles all the way through an infinite multiplicity of expressions, all of our karmically limited experiences are directly connected to more subtle and expansive expressions. We can follow the thread and arrive at a bigger View and more freedom.

My sticky, grabby love for a single person is universal love for all people under tension. Under the force of sadhana, my body, energy, and mind can relax. Virtue can unfold and find its larger expression.

My overweening self-concern is concern for the well-being of all under tension. My craving for sweets is the same longing to taste the sweetness of all existence. My undiscerning devotion to a very limited teacher is that clear devotion further down the road, but just under tension.

Anandamayi Ma said:

> *In the world, everybody's mad about something or the other; some more, some to a lesser extent. See, God's play (lila) is so enjoyable. He has created a madhouse. Try to find yourself through yourself.*[8]

In every act and every thought, we are expressing the fundamental wisdoms of enlightened essence nature. With the right help and good methods, you can always find yourself through yourself.

19

God is both the limited and the unlimited

Limited, relative experience and the absolute always come together. Only the revelation of the whole is self-realization.

Relative or limited experience means our ordinary experience in dualistic karmic vision. We are conditioned by concepts, by limited desires, and by our attachment to linear time. Relative experience begins with anavamala, our experience of separation.

Relative teachings and relative View help us to navigate our life as beings experiencing separation, birth, death, and suffering. For instance, we can observe precepts and take vows in order to regulate our conduct and conserve energy. We can try to do no harm to ourselves and others. We learn not to put our hand in fire or try to walk through a wall.

Absolute experience is enlightened experience. It means that we much more fully and consciously embody our real, unconditioned nature. We are not so bound by habit patterns or by attachment to linear time and concepts of space. Our activity is skillful, spontaneous, and uncontrived. We are being immersed in presence and have direct knowledge of the wisdom of the natural state. Absolute teachings and View relate to the ultimate nature of reality.

You may assume that the goal of sadhana is to leave the relative behind and "ascend" to a version of the absolute in which all differentiation is erased. In fact, sometimes when people hear nondual teachings, they try to ignore relative experience. This is called spiritual bypassing.

As long as you continue to experience separation, you'll have to deal with the experience of suffering. You are going to have to deal with pain, disappointment, frustration, and failure. Dressing in white, chastising your senses, talking a good nondual line, and attempting to "rise" above it all does not change these basic facts. If a truck is heading toward you, and you don't get out of the way, it *will* hit you.

You cannot ignore dualistic karmic vision, but under the force of sadhana, you can begin to experience the manifest world differently. From the perspective of View, the everyday and the esoteric are equally made by and of enlightened consciousness and energy. Relative and absolute are entwined. There is nothing to reject. A pile of poop is no less God than a sadhu. In India, you sometimes see people doing puja to fresh cow dung, or you come across offerings of flowers laid atop dung. It is very beautiful.

Doing consistent sadhana, we can begin to experience the limited world as an aspect or expression of enlightened essence nature. Our experience of body, energy, and mind begins to transform. Our level of suffering can subside even as we enjoy the experience of difference. But we are not leaving anything behind other than our suffering.

Realization does not leave anything out. As Anandamayi Ma said:
> A state had been described where everything is burnt and only the One remains, so that even when searching for diversity one cannot find it anymore; everything has disappeared into the One. It means that some aspect is still in darkness, for this is not

> *Self-Revelation... When pure consciousness has been attained the image will be known as the Essence Itself.*[9]

When the image, when things, and beings, and worlds are known as Essence Itself, then the Self stands revealed. But as long as we are still busy rejecting and accepting, even rejecting dualistic vision, we are still in darkness.

Most of the View and practices we learn are aimed at helping us to work with our relative condition. We have to learn how to take care of our bodies; use our energy properly; recognize and release karmic patterns of body, emotions, and mind; and relate more skillfully to others. If we do not take care of the relative, it is much harder to realize. We may unnecessarily enter into a condition of self-neglect, or we may engage with others in ways that divert our energy and attention and delay or degrade our sadhana.

One of the human world's great disciples, Jyotish Chandra Roy, said this:

> *On this life's journey, keep attending to your own steps. As you come nearer and nearer the destination, you will find yourself reconciled not only to the Ideal, but also, most difficult of all, to others.*[10]

In some spiritual traditions, students are taught relative View first. If they stick around and continue to practice, they are eventually taught Absolute View. In the direct realization traditions, the teaching method is different. Students are first taught Absolute, or Supreme View and, nearly at the same time, relative View.

The method of offering written teachings in the Trika tradition is similar. When we read a Tantra or other teaching text, the first teaching in the book is all-encompassing. If you can "get" that teaching, there is no need to read the rest of the text. Of course, nearly everyone needs to read it all!

More subtle practices are also given first, along with more concrete and accessible practices. The idea of this teaching method is that we are all in different conditions. Each person is a unique and infinite event. If a person can realize the most subtle teaching at the beginning, they should have an opportunity to do that. We can always "fall back."

More importantly, the Absolute serves as a beacon and the biggest "container" for our lives and practice even when we are far from realizing it for ourselves. Knowing Absolute View helps us to not get stuck. For students in direct realization traditions, the trick is to keep the bigger View in mind as we work with our limited condition. When we remember the Absolute in the context of our everyday lives, we are not taking things so personally. We are eroding our sense of self-importance and overheated self-concern. We are less likely to get stuck. So even for students with many obscurations, there is benefit in hearing of the Supreme reality, your own real nature.

20

Ignorance of your real nature is the cause of suffering

Suffering is the absence of access to wisdom, not the presence of sin or fault.

One of the names of Lord Shiva, reality itself, is "the Auspicious." When you do a lot of spiritual practice, you discover the essential wisdom and goodness of existence. You discover that reality is flooded with and made of wisdom virtues. These wisdom virtues are capacities such as compassion, mercy, kindness, tenderness, clarity, curiosity, intelligence, creativity, generosity, and playfulness.

Because there is only wisdom, we cannot properly talk of evil or sin. All of the acts we might call evil, sinful, or simply disturbed arise from anavamala, our experience of separation. When you are mired in the experience of being a body with space around you, when your own energy and mind feel isolated, when you have the understanding that you were born and are going to die, you are embodying anavamala. You have temporarily forgotten your real circumstance, what you actually are.

Our experience of separation gives rise to all loneliness,

defensiveness, aggression, and attachment. If you firmly believe that you are this single person, you are going to defend your territory. You are going to try to resolve the "problem" of your loneliness and fragility. We do this by fighting off perceived attacks and clinging to whatever it is we feel will ameliorate our condition: other people or animals, possessions, food, power, and acclaim. This is suffering.

Anavamala comes in degrees. If you were a rock, you would still be made of enlightened essence nature. But that reality, out of its own creative freedom, has fashioned you with a high degree of anavamala. You would be very, very ignorant of your real nature. By the time we get to the portion of the continuum of becoming that is inhabited by dogs and crows, we can clearly see the ability to self-reflect.

Human beings host an enormously varied range of capacities to self-reflect and become more aware. Some people have no inkling that there is any kind of experience outside of their own limited perspective. They feel extremely separate. Others have an unstoppable desire to find out about reality and to be of service.

The experience of suffering relates to a natural and temporary limitation in our capacity to connect with the larger Self. It is an aspect of dualistic karmic vision. Yet all limitation is also the play of the one Self. The light of consciousness shows up as both the play of ignorance and the play of waking up.

One time, a father came to satsang. He had two daughters. One daughter had been murdered, the other raped. He was so enraged and distraught, he had to be hospitalized for a time and remained heavily medicated. He lost interest in his work and lost his job. His life was in a shambles.

During the course of several satsangs, he asked many questions. He was sincerely looking for a way out of pain. Among many other exchanges, at one point I related to him that I had been raped by a stranger as a young teenager. I was very upset, of course, but I never felt angry. I did not feel victimized.

At the time, I thought this was strange. I searched and searched within myself to make sure that I was not in a state of denial. After all, we are told over and over again that when a person is violently raped, that experience is supposed to cause lasting damage. But I did not feel damaged.

I finally came to the conclusion that I had not experienced the person who raped me as having actually done it specifically to me. I recognized that he was in the grip of compulsion. I could have been anyone. There was nothing personal about the act. Even at that time, I realized that raping and violence was on a continuum with many other kinds of harm. I wanted it all to stop, including whatever harm had come to this man that had left him in such a dark condition. I actually felt that he was much worse off than I was, in spite of the rape.

The father slowly started to understand that the world didn't have it in for him or his daughters. Even if someone says they want to hurt you, specifically you, they are in the grip of karmic tension. If you were not there, they would find another "you." When you start to dis-identify with your own karma, you begin to see more clearly how people are trapped in karmic habit patterns over which they often have little control.

The father also started to experience compassion for the people who had harmed his daughters. Instead of feeling that everyone involved was either a victim or evil, he began to understand that we are all in the same boat. He also understood that he and his daughters were not being punished. They were not being "paid back." There was no sin, or fault, or blame to go around.

After some months, he left a more relaxed person. His relief was palpable, and this brought tears to everyone's eyes. He had opened up to more of an experience of continuity, and his suffering was at least somewhat alleviated. This is an example of the relative nature of suffering and how opening to a wider View, a.k.a. greater wisdom, relieves suffering.

21

There is no suffering

Our life dramas are actual stories. Enjoyment, not suffering, is the foundation of existence.

We humans spend an absolutely enormous amount of our time engaged in telling stories, making stories, contemplating stories, and enjoying stories. We wake up in the morning and tell ourselves or a housemate stories about what happened yesterday, or about a dream we had, or about the day ahead. We turn on the news and listen to stories. Or perhaps we look at Facebook and read stories and then watch a story or two on YouTube.

If we spend our days talking to people, we are likely creating scenarios, planning, and telling stories about ourselves. When we are not speaking stories, we are narrating stories about the past, present, and future in our minds. Some of us make a living telling stories!

We get home and tell some more stories about our day, or about our thoughts and emotions. Then we watch stories on TV. Then we read stories to our kids. Then we go to sleep and dream stories all night long.

Maybe on the weekend we go to a play or a movie, or we visit with friends and share more stories. We go on a trip or a hike, and after we return, we have a lot of stories to tell about the relatively brief time when we were actually just experiencing something and not telling a story. If we are writers or painters or dancers or some other kind of artist, we have even more vehicles for telling stories.

Many of our stories are shaped by tensions and karmic patterns. They painfully repeat over and over again. The way we talk, our gestures, facial expressions, and other modes of communication often tell habitual stories and are part of our self-image formation. Occasionally we play more lightly and spontaneously with ourselves and our stories. We call this fun or art. We love contemplating ourselves through the experience of storytelling.

Why do we supposed-adults spend such an astounding amount of time engaged in creating stories? Because this is what God does. As above, so below. Everything in continuity, all the way through. Reality is simple this way.

We tell our stories. And God is "telling" us. We are God's art, God's drama, God's creative self-expressions.

So how does this relate to suffering?

Nothing is really happening here other than a literal play of creative wisdom. "Play means both "playfulness" and "drama." So there is actually no suffering. This is the absolute teaching. How can we understand this?

When you watch a movie, you are seeing a play of light and energy that has been shaped by creative intelligence. You know that. So you can enjoy tragedy, murder, mayhem, and destruction. You can enjoy crying and feeling really scared.

When you leave the movie theater or turn away from your TV and walk out into the world, you are also seeing an intelligent, creative play of light and energy. You have just forgotten that.

Step out of ordinary mind for a moment. Contemplate just how weird it is that we enjoy all this painful, scary stuff in the movies.

If it's so bad in "real life," why would we want to re-live it in the movies?

When we go to the movies, or to a play, or other performance, we are contemplating ourselves. We are appreciating our creativity and imagination. We are appreciating our own nature as human beings. This is what God does with the 'story' that is all of manifest life.

Manifest life is a display of the Supreme by the Supreme with all parts played by the Supreme. This alive, aware subjectivity is contemplating and enjoying its nature in the same way that we do. At the movies we are able to recognize this, and so we don't really suffer. Even more impressive, we can "try on" suffering and enjoy its flavors.

In a real sense, we are like actors on a set. We have the capacity to enjoy playing all kinds of roles and to see others play them. If we are actors in drama, we can enjoy playing characters with limitations: someone who is inept at relating to other people and has divorced a lot of times or someone with a deadly disease. It is so much fun!

But one day, we forget that these roles are being played by actors. We suddenly believe that we really *are* those characters. Then everything becomes very serious, and instead of enjoying ourselves, we are suffering. This is our normal condition.

Swami Lakshmanjoo, the great 20th century teacher of Trika Shaivism, wrote in his commentary on Vasgupta's *Shiva Sutras*:

> In this field of drama, the actor is your own nature, your own self of universal consciousness. This self of universal consciousness is the one who is aware, he is the actor in this universal drama. Those who are not aware are not actors; they are played in this drama. They experience sadness, they experience enjoyment, they become joyful, they become depressed. But those who are aware, they are always elevated; they are the real players in this drama.[11]

The journey of the *sadhika*, the practitioner, is from the played to the player, from one who has forgotten to one who remembers. Upon remembering, we can more consciously participate in the *lila*, the sport or the play of the divine.

You will probably wonder at some point: what about compassion? What about kindness? If all suffering is relative to dualistic experience, and the foundation is enjoyment, why bother being kind or helping anyone?

There is no sense in which we hear "there is no suffering" and then repeat that with a superior air next time a friend approaches us with a problem. We are also not going to ignore our own suffering in an attempt to be "spiritual."

It is hard for students to remember this, but everything is already made of and full of virtue. Wisdom virtues, such as compassion and kindness, are built into the fabric of reality. Shiva Nature is goodness without an opposite.

On the level of relative experience, the more you wake up, the more you will naturally express these wisdom virtues effortlessly. Highly realized people are more compassionate and kind, not less. Embodying the recognition of your real nature and the real nature of everything is equal to embodying all wisdom virtues more fully.

We get caught up here because in our relative condition, we believe there has to be a reason to be compassionate and kind. If that reason is taken away, seemingly by the teaching that there is no suffering, then we become afraid. We cannot imagine unmotivated compassion and kindness. This is *our* limitation.

But the universal Self needs no reason to express compassion. Compassion is its nature, and it expresses its own nature without restraint in all circumstances. Our job is to rediscover that.

22

Manifest life is a cascade of becoming and unbecoming

Manifest life continually emerges from the heart of the Supreme Self in an effulgent cascade of becoming and unbecoming that has no up or down, no beginning and no end.

Imagine a vast, shining, horizontal field. From that arise and subside an infinite number of forms. These forms can be more subtle or more gross, more expansive or contracted, more expressive of wisdom or less. This arising and subsiding continues everywhere, throughout all time. It is the never-ending life process of the Absolute.

The cascade of becoming and unbecoming is not an origin story that starts at a point in time and eventually comes to an end point. Although represented vertically when visualized during a traditional teaching, it is not vertical. The field of becoming and unbecoming is alive everywhere all at once.

Tattva means element. The thirty-six, or sometimes thirty-seven tattvas, as described in the Trika teachings are experiential potentials or capacities that emerge from the totally unconditioned, alive and aware base state of infinite potential. These capacities ultimately produce experiences of the five great elements: space, wind, fire, water, and earth. These in turn give rise to the most condensed forms such as planets, stars, you, me, cars, and rocks. I refer to this as a cascade because, at a time when I was doing intense sadhana, I had a waking vision of the powerful, magnificent overflow of the creation from its heart. It filled my entire field of vision, and it appeared as a moving cascade.

The cascade begins with the unconditioned and its complete freedom to create experiences out of the play of self-limitation. Consider hearing. We humans and many other creatures have organs of hearing: our ears. Ears are tangible. They appear to be made of dense material. They are what we commonly call things.

Your physical ears are a gross manifestation of the more subtle, less localized capacity of this alive, aware reality to produce sound and the experience of hearing. Our condensed, limited ears emerge or are emitted through a cascade of becoming that begins with the primordial Self's most subtle, expansive, and pervasive capacity to sound and to hear.

The primordial power to sound and to experience hearing is less conditioned and more generalized than hearing a particular sound with a particular organ. It is the universal sounding and hearing of reality itself present everywhere.

As we move along the cascade of becoming toward the more limited and conditioned, we eventually bump into you and your strong conviction that you need your physical ears to hear. You are conditioned by this embodied belief. Just as it is difficult for people to let go of any entrenched habit, it is difficult for most people to let go of their fixed idea about ears and to listen without the support of their physical ears.

But every ordinary person hears sound in dreams. Where is this sound? Where is it coming from? And what organ is hearing this sound? Even if you believe that the sound in dreams and the organ of hearing in your dreams is the brain, you can understand that this "brain sound" and those "brain ears" are more subtle and less conditioned than the sounds you hear and the ears you hear with when you are awake.

In your dream, you can hear sounds that are fanciful and are not occurring in your physical environment. If you are good at dream yoga, the practice of aware dreaming, you might even be able to control what sounds you hear in your dreams.

But when you are awake, you cannot hear a tropical bird singing in the tree outside of your home in North America in the dead of winter. You cannot make any sound appear just by willing it to appear. Your waking life is more conditioned by your embodied concepts of reality.

In fact, yogis discover that our literal ears are not our organs of hearing. Our ears are living symbols of an aware, awake reality's capacity in general to produce sound and experiences of sound. More realized yogis can hear, not only the gross sounds of every day, but more subtle sounds, for instance inner sounds from the subtle body and sounds from far away and from more subtle realms of existence.

It is not even so uncommon that people whose senses are naturally a little more open, or who have done some spiritual practice, are able to receive instruction or teachings via subtle speech and subtle hearing. You may have had this experience yourself when you heard an inner voice giving you wise instruction or urging you to take or avoid a certain course of action.

All of our sense organs, including our minds, are gateways to more subtle sensing. They emerge from the tattvas, capacities that sit behind and give rise to experiences of physical form. As we subtilize our senses, we rediscover less conditioned intelligence, less conditioned insight, and less conditioned compassion. We reconnect our perceptual and expressive capacities back to the universal.

23

Maya makes diversity for the Lord

Maya is the sculptress and the sorceress. She carves out worlds with the knives of time and unknowing.

In *Sankhya*, the ancient dualistic tradition of India, and in the nondual, more transcendental Hindu traditions, Maya is most often translated as "illusion." According to these Views, Maya is the Shakti, the power, that causes us to mistake this world for the Absolute. She is feared and even reviled for this reason. Maya is a temptress, luring us away from God with shiny, unreal objects of desire.

The Vedic and Tantrik associations with Maya are "art," "magic," and "power." These get closer to the role of Maya in Trika Shaivism. Maya wields Shiva's power of self-limitation. She is the weaver and the artist. The tools of Maya Devi are the five *kanchukas*, or forms of self-limitation on the experience of the fullness of the Absolute.

Kalā is limited action.

Vidya is limited knowledge.

Raga is the limitation of the feeling of completeness.
Kalā is the experience of linear time, of being subject to birth and death.
Niyati is the limitation on omnipresence.

In the Trika, Maya is she who creates the wild diversity of beings, worlds, and circumstances. She uses her tools, the kanchukas, much like the sculptor or the ceramist. She carves out the infinite displays of the manifest from the unconditioned via limitations on time, understanding, the feeling of completeness, omnipresence, and power. She is the cosmic creative force that shapes the overflowing and unstoppable impulse to self-express. Maya is sometimes called "the weaver of the garb" because she "costumes" unconditioned Shiva Nature and causes it to appear in diverse forms.

Maya also inaugurates the entire play of sadhana. Our perception of our own limitations, our feeling of incompletion, and the longing to encounter the limitless drive us to seek teachers and teachings and to undertake spiritual practice. This is the grand game of Shiva-Shakti. There is enjoyment in the experience of separation and in finding one's way back to self-understanding and union. And so reality enacts the play of sadhana with a little help from the powerful Maya Shakti.

24

All is perfection

Everything here is a perfect expression of living awareness. True, false, right, and wrong do not apply.

On a relative level, if a truck is headed toward us, we try to get out of the way. If we are taking an arithmetic test, we want to answer that 2+2=4. If a door is closed, and we want to pass through to another room, we open the door. We can't walk through the closed door, and we wouldn't bash it in with a sledgehammer. That would bring unwanted consequences such as repair bills and possibly eviction. In general, we cannot ignore these aspects of relative, dualistic experience.

These are some of the practical moves we make in order to navigate our lives here in samsara. But many times we are not so practical.

We complain endlessly about other people's behavior and about difficult circumstances. We find it "wrong" or even "evil" when people do not conform to certain standards of behavior established by us or our societies. We find fault with natural disasters and rail at God. We celebrate when people behave as we wish and expect, when the weather is good, or when our good works are recognized.

We experience outrage when people disagree with truths we feel are evident or when they criticize us. We feel comfortable and confirmed when we are surrounded by those who agree with us.

The complaints and celebrations, the outrage and confirmations, all are aspects of suffering. Our feeling of being okay is at the mercy of ever-shifting circumstances. We are leading fragile, uneven lives ping-ponging between feel good, feel bad, approve, and disapprove.

When we have first-hand experience of essence nature, we come to understand that everything in manifest life is *that* showing up as a person, a car, a building, or a circumstance. Every manifestation in our relative experience is the play of God with God playing every role. So on an Absolute level, everything is perfect. Everything is goodness without an opposite.

"Truth" as applied to reality itself is nonsensical. You would not walk up to a tree and declare it "true" or "false." That would not make any sense. Even if a tree were ill or deformed, you would not declare it "evil" or "wrong."

People are no different from trees. All manifest life is the self-expression of an aware, alive reality. A painting may be more or less sophisticated. A tree may be healthy or diseased. A spiritual tradition may have a narrow or a wide view, but they are all equally expressions of wisdom. Even a lie is a real expression of God. Everything and everyone is acting their part perfectly. In a real way, everything is a perfect expression of that Supreme Self. When we understand this, we can develop abiding appreciation and respect for others.

Many people naturally want to have something like "truth" to hold onto, but truth and falsity are always relative. Here, Swami Lakshmanjoo explains Abhinavagupta's teaching on the real nature of the svatantrya: the unconditioned freedom of self-expression that is enjoyed by God.

> The greatest svātantrya (independence) of Lord Śiva is durgha a sa pādana: [that] which is possible, that becomes impossible; [that] which is impossible, that becomes possible.[12]

If the possible can become impossible and the impossible possible, where does "truth" lie?

Unfortunately, the word *Sat* in Sanskrit is very often mistranslated as "truth." Sat does not mean truth. It connotes existence, presence, endurance, authenticity, and goodness. People reading teachings often get the wrong impression that we are supposed to be looking for the truth when in fact we are being pointed toward immersion in natural, usable wisdom.

As practitioners, we are holding the relative and the Absolute together. We act practically and effectively on a relative level while making an effort to base our experience in the Absolute. We are not trying to bypass the relative.

As a navigational tool, it is extremely useful to remember that whatever ideas of truth and falsity or right and wrong you are hanging onto, there can always be an otherwise. Your truth is someone else's falsity. A cultural or political "truth," and especially religious "truths," are highly contested around the globe. Even the so-called laws of physics do not apply in every circumstance. And then, what about other universes? Perhaps in some place, objects fall upward and time runs backwards. Who knows?

With this understanding, we can stop relating to circumstances through emotional hysteria and dogmatism. We can be more compassionate and more skillful. We can be better listeners. We won't build so many walls.

25

Recognize, gain confidence, and immerse yourself in presence

There is no path, but while we are enjoying the relative experience of a path, we can benefit from a map.

Pratyabhijña is most often translated as "recognition." The Pratyabhijña school is one of the Kashmiri spiritual traditions that came to be included in the View of what we now call Trika Shaivism or Shaiva Tantra. During the late 9th century to early 11th century, Somananda, his disciple Utpaladeva, Abhinavagupta, and his disciple Kshemaraja wrote the texts that became the foundation of the modern understanding of pratyabhijña.[13]

Pratyabhijña means to recognize your real nature, or the nature of reality. Recognizing your real nature does not mean to discover something for the first time. You are actually re-discovering or remembering.

Recognition is necessary to begin direct realization sadhana. This may happen spontaneously, but more usually it happens in the context of your relationship to a teacher and a practice. Through the alchemy of transmission, the teacher and the practice re-introduce you to your real nature. This can happen many times over before you recognize.

Recognition is not discovering something new. It is also not an intellectual recognition or understanding. You also cannot permanently refuse to recognize. Recognition of your real nature is an inevitability, in this life or another. As Utpaladeva writes: "Sovereignty is established through inner awareness. Therefore only the foolish strive to establish or deny the Lord."[14]

In other words, the Supreme is already established as an inner awareness. The capacity to recognize and what is to be recognized are "built-in" from the beginning. Karmic conditioning obscures this inner awareness like the clouds obscure the sun. But the awareness is always there in full measure. Trying to prove or create an experience of the Supreme intellectually, or denying the existence of the Supreme, or blocking its announcement, are foolish operations. Ultimately, the Supreme will be victorious.

Any committed student of a direct realization tradition understands that the response of recognition is provoked in the heart and is drawn out of the heart. We receive transmission and teachings. We hear about our real nature. At some point, perhaps right away, perhaps not, there is a deep, spontaneous response of recognition. This can happen in the midst of doubt, seeming lack of interest, or even skepticism. It is as if the teacher and the teachings are the forever friends of the Supreme, and *that* calls out with wild gladness from within to meet them.

Once recognition sounds in the heart, the path truly begins. Without recognition, you don't know where you are going or how to proceed. Recognition relates to the direct realization strategy of beginning with the end, or taking the fruit for the path. With recognition, you have a beacon. You can find your way.

Recognition is often not steady or strong at first; it can come and go. We remember and forget, remember and forget again. Our recognition is not firm. The coming and going leaves room for doubt.

Now we must use our sadhana and our teacher to become confident in the recognition of our real nature, the nature of all. We must, as Utpaladeva writes, acquire "unswerving certainty."[15]

I have often compared this process to wading into deeper and deeper water. At first we are in the shallow end. We only recognize what is happening at the surface. We are only half-way in. We walk into deeper waters as we continue to practice.

For instance, being with our teacher, we may feel a sweetness and lightness and sense of relaxation mixed with the poignancy of homecoming after having been lost. We may have different kinds of energetic and emotional experiences that call into question the nature of our bodies and minds and help us to feel less separate. These are all "shallow-end" experiences, but they are important aspects of recognition.

More dramatic experiences of deepening our recognition, and therefore our certainty, will occur. But despite talk of sudden enlightenment, for most people, immersion is not something accomplished like diving from dry ground into deep ocean. It appears to approach us slowly. This is because our senses are not open enough at first to recognize wisdom on such a grand scale. As our senses subtilize, remembrance of our real nature becomes deeper and more experientially continuous.

At some point we also recognize that there is no inside and no outside. Our real nature is unbroken and infinite. This is when our entrance into the experience of samavesha, or immersion truly begins. After some years or lifetimes, the vastness and fountain-like quality of the wisdom heart reveals itself everywhere.

That eternal, infinite Self is your real nature. Because it is what you are, you can and will inevitably come to experientially know it and reintegrate your individualized experience with that. The openhearted, overflowing virtue and skillful action that arise as a result of reintegrating with the natural state are the ultimate fruits of practice.

26

Guru is the View, the method, and the fruit

Without Guru and transmission, there is no way out of ignorance.

Guru is not merely a person. In Trika Shaivism, we have the possibility to directly experience that the Guru tattva, or Guru element, is present everywhere. Individual Gurus are instances of that pervasive and unerring clarity, wisdom, and force of desire that moves beings toward awakening.

Our longing for self-understanding is Guru. The actions we take to seek knowledge of reality are Guru. Guru fuels spiritual paths and lineages, and Guru is the creator of those. Guru is embodied in every true teacher. Guru is the call of our own hearts leading us step-by-step toward wisdom. Guru is the signs and instructions we begin to notice everywhere as our perceptions open. Guru is a function, a power, a process, and many people. There is no path without Guru, and Guru is the path.

The central practice of direct realization Tantra is working with a human being who has direct knowledge of the natural state and who can convey that to you via a process called "transmission." Transmission means that through the alchemy of your relationship to the teacher, you can have a real experience of your essence nature. Transmission does not mean that the teacher is giving you energy, or something you lack. You already have the same enlightened essence nature as the teacher. And actually, that is the transmission.

Without transmission, you likely will not have a clear experience of what it is you are trying to realize. Transmission is a beacon you can follow. Doing sadhana is how you follow that beacon and enlarge your capacity to recognize and remain in the natural state. So the teacher is responsible for re-introducing you to living presence, and you are responsible for doing practice and making immersion in that your new normal.

The teacher also imparts the View and knows some methods you can use to come to embody the View. These are methods that the teacher has already practiced and realized. The best teachers embody the View to such an extent that their very way of being in the world is a powerful teaching. Finally, the teacher acts as a mirror, showing you where you are stuck, and helping you to get unstuck. Because we have many attachments, we are unlikely to do this for ourselves. We need help!

Guru is a natural technology for waking up. What sparks your curiosity about spiritual paths? What causes you to look for some kind of practice to do? It is that wisdom that is coming to you through the heart chakra. Through that gateway, Guru is calling out, waiting patiently for you to listen.

Guru awakens the longing for a teacher and makes that longing grow stronger and stronger until you find one. And that same wisdom allows you to follow the instructions of the teacher and experience some sort of confidence in what's going on even if it is outside of your frame of reference.

Anandamayi Ma said:

The Guru resides in your own heart, but most people are unable

> *to rely firmly on their own self, so they have to take refuge in an external Guru. But in actual fact, the Guru resides within one's own heart.*[16]

We have a sense of inner knowing that is more durable and insistent than any convention, emotional need, fixation, intellect, or circumstance. Those people who are ripe will be able to hear and listen to that inner knowing in spite of criticism or doubts. When we have that capacity and follow the promptings of our wisdom heart, that's when we encounter Guru.

People reject Gurus for various reasons, or they say they are following inner Guru even when they have little experience of essence nature. The first stage is not bypassing Guru. The first stage is to set out on a path that eventually leads you to recognize that having help is good. The fact is, when you are a little awake, you really want help!

In order to realize continuity, you first need to understand the value of being in alliance with others in our world. Much of the time, we value a gross kind of independence, a crass kind of freedom. But there is really not very much independence or freedom to be found in following your fixations without resistance!

The Guru will try to help you to surrender your attachments, your rigidity, your contrivances, your emotional patterns, your fixed ideas about life, and your self concepts. In effect, you are surrendering your brand. The result is that you will eventually live totally immersed in living presence, experiencing clarity, spontaneity, and freshness in your body, energy, and mind. Despite this great result, you will fight the entire way to hang onto limitation. Guru, in whatever form it takes, is here to make sure that freedom is victorious.

Sometimes you read or hear that you have to see Guru as God. People really take this the wrong way. Even some "Gurus" capitalize on the misunderstanding of this teaching. People assume it means you must put Guru on a pedestal above the merely human. This is dead wrong.

Realization means you have to see God in everything, without exception, not just the bits of life you consider to be "spiritual" or "holy." Guru is your training for that. If you put Guru on a pedestal, just be sure you know that the pedestal is also God. Whether your teacher is spouting profundities, or picking their nose, God is present.

First you have to reconcile yourself to both the ordinary and the extraordinary in your teacher, and then in everyone. Ultimately, you have to experience *that* creative intelligence in all manifestations of life. The binary of ordinary and extraordinary, or mundane and spiritual, is a booby prize. There is magic everywhere.

If you want to experience God in everyone and everything, you have to actually experience God. And if you want to experience God, you have to do a lot of sadhana. You have to wear away the tyranny of your ordinary perceptions, the tyranny of your ordinary senses that only see and hear the most gross things. You have to subtilize yourself. You can't just wander around inanely repeating that everyone is God. Self-realization is not an idea or a proclamation.

In the *Guru Stotram* it says: *Salutations to that glorious Guru, who, when I was blinded by ignorance, applied medicine and opened my eyes.*

We work with human teachers because we are trying to fully explore and realize the full potential of being human. Only human teachers can help us to do that. They are the medicine that helps us to see perfection in all of the messiness of life without exception.

27

Lose the watcher

God is not a watcher; God is a contemplator and an enjoyer.

Imagine yourself in a pleasing landscape. It might be a mountain meadow, a forest glade, a lake shore, or quiet inlet cove. You are enjoying the smells, the sights, the sounds, and the feeling of the air moving around you. You are immersed in the scene. You are not standing back, analyzing it from the position of a pair of abstract, intellectual eyes. Your natural intelligence and your senses drink deeply of the total circumstance, going out to meet it, and being met in return. You experience immediacy. You feel relaxed, alive, and integrated with Nature.

In some spiritual traditions, students are advised to take up the stance of a watcher with respect to their thoughts and emotions, or even life in general. God in some systems is defined as a watcher. These traditions are dualistic. Dualism is performed by the repeatedly marking three poles of perception: the seer, the act of seeing, and the seen.

By internally adopting the position of the watcher, dualistic experience is made even stronger. Whether you are watching your thoughts or everything, you must split yourself into the watcher and the watched. The watcher takes up a disembodied, bird's eye view.

Unfortunately, Western psychology only makes matters worse. The psychological View of a person teaches us that our thoughts, and particularly our emotions, are of utmost importance and deeply problematic. The result has been that generations of people not only experience thoughts and emotions, but also pathologize a good portion of their experience. They syphon lots of energy into thinking about thoughts, feeling about feelings, and feeling badly about how they think and feel. This relentless enterprise of self-concern and self-repair proceeds in deadly earnest.

In direct realization Tantra, the goal is to lose the watcher. The watcher is understood to be a contrivance that propagates dualistic experience and requires undue effort to maintain. For this reason, practices in direct realization traditions do not emphasize activities such as watching the breath or the thoughts. We are not so interested in examining the mind. We are simply resting in the natural state as much as we can. This dissolves karmic habit patterns of thoughts and emotions much more quickly and thoroughly than distanced, analytic, restrained, or combative stances toward ourselves.

Limited emotions and thoughts are patterns of consciousness and energy. We don't need to attack or fight our emotions or our mind. When we identify and integrate with the natural state, we can recognize the real nature of thoughts and feelings. As we begin to experience their real nature, they lose their ability to distract or rule us. As thoughts and emotions come and go, we remain, contemplating and enjoying our own nature everywhere.

28

The mind is the organ of curiosity

From within every cell of our bodies and every subtle channel, the mind excites the exploration of all.

Our relationship to mind—our minds and *the* mind—radically transforms over the course of engaging in practices such as meditation and mantra. We may bring to our practice received, strong associations of the mind with analytic thinking, theorizing, and information processing. We also may relate to our minds as the seat of psychology. Minds in this paradigm are a storehouse of thoughts, memories, and emotional patterns. Many of us are taught to believe that mind is produced by and is located in the brain.

Over the course of sadhana, we eventually come to experience mind as a sense organ and as immanent to all of our senses. We discover mind in every cell in our bodies and in the channels of our subtle energy body. We will develop the capacity to directly experience mind impelling all of the senses to reach into life and to learn to converse with life's diverse circumstances from the most gross to the most subtle.

When we contact living presence using our real intelligence, we are entering into the experience of a dialog that ultimately teaches us about the nature of reality. It is this mind, along with all of our other senses, that relaxes its boundaries in order to be receptive to the reintegration with all of life. In the best circumstance, mind is always being in a condition of freshness and awakeness. Just as when we are conversing with someone, we want them to be listening in an open and undistracted way, so our minds are ideally listening undistractedly to whatever is arriving.

Natural intelligence is without any defensiveness or aggression. It receives impressions and reaches out to meet what is coming toward it as you would listen to a beautiful, subtle piece of music. You are not making anything of it in an aggressive way; you are letting the music reveal itself to you. At the same time, you are not passive. You are actively engaged with the music, as if you and the music were dance partners.

In the direct realization traditions, we are trying to be integrated with presence. We have the View that karmically patterned thoughts and emotions will unwind more quickly by integrating with presence than they will by doing other effortful things to try to control ordinary mind. Just continue your sadhana, trying to recognize and integrate with essence nature. You can begin to experience your real intelligence, set free to listen, feel, and explore reality. In our overly psychologized cultures, sometimes it is best to begin with listening. Listening moves the awareness out of the hothouses of our emotional lives. But eventually, you only need to be in a condition of receptivity and active, open-ended curiosity.

29

The relative purpose of life is self-realization

There is nothing to accomplish. Everything is already awake and totally free from the beginning.

You might think that self-realization is a serious, lofty goal. You might have the idea that as a practitioner you are doing something very important. You have practiced hard, and you now you have more clarity. You feel more compassion for people. You are able to help people more skillfully. You feel your life has meaning because you are waking up. This is wonderful. It is a marvelous experience, thrilling even. But self-realization is the play of essence nature expressing itself. While the play of Lord Shiva is thrilling, you are not actually accomplishing anything. In fact, there is nothing to accomplish.

The whole journey, from the first inkling that there might be more to life, all the way through to enlightenment, is built into nature, into the life process of Shiva-Shakti. Shiva-Shakti creates many experiences of limited forms of life. All of them are playing a huge game. The purpose of the game is to walk backward from ignorance to once again experience the delight of who you really are.

Your life is like a long TV series. You have the little episodic stories that change each week, but then you have the arc story. Self-realization is the arc story. But nothing has really happened. The Lord is not journeying toward wisdom; the Lord is wisdom. The play of a journey is enacted purely for the sake of enjoyment. The actors have just played their parts.

Earnestness is one of the major spiritual diseases that afflicts practitioners and teachers alike. The news that the entire journey from the experience of relative ignorance to self-realization is God's play should not dismay you. Nor should you think, "Well, if that's the case, I refuse to participate!"

The game of waking up is the best story arc around, full of chills, thrills, spills, infinite surprise turns, and a blockbuster ending. It's the greatest romance, mystery, space opera, and indie mind bender of all times all rolled into one. Bottom line: There is no form of life that will ask more of your intelligence, your creativity, your sensitivity, and your heart. Nor will any other form of life give you such wealth in return. Well, except here's a spoiler: what really happens is that you find out that you already possessed that wealth all along. Like I said, blockbuster ending.

But the real kicker is: you can't help yourself. It doesn't matter what arguments your mind makes or resistance your karma lobs at your aspirations to realize. You *will* seek greater continuity. You're already doing it in every aspect of your activity, including reading this book. You *will* try to learn more about who you really are and what's going on here. And you will find out.

Despite my Guru's profound understanding of the absolute nature of reality, she spent her entire life teaching and exhorting people to do sadhana. She talked over and over again about the importance of a daily practice and of keeping one's mind focused on the divine every minute of the day. Why? Because this is what is happening here. This is what we do. And if we are going to play this game, we may as well play it with gusto.

The purpose, or really the process, of realizing is already built into impermanent, relative existence. You already had a job and a job description from the moment you got here. That is good news, actually. Because you can stop worrying about the purpose of your life.

If anyone wants to know why you are a practitioner, or why you are a teacher, the only real answer is because this is what God does. There is nothing to develop pride around. If we do develop pride about our spiritual life, that is also just a flavor of the game. Knowing this, we can work with our relative condition and be as earnest as we like. But we can and should always maintain a small secret smile about it all, and occasionally, actually as often as possible, laugh really hard at our absurd and wonderful predicament.

30

Duality is for the enjoyment of reciprocity

We live in a devotional, call-and-response world.

Right now, I am writing to you. I am having a kind of conversation with you. It is enjoyable. All manifest life is engaged in what the Sufi poet Rumi described as a "constant conversation."[17] The hallmark of dualistic experience is that we are having the constant experience of being in contact with that which appears to be separate from us. Being in conversation with others, with nature, and with circumstances can be the source of suffering, but it is also our greatest pleasure. The degree to which social networks magnetize our attention testifies to this.

Dualistic experience is a total theater in which everything is meeting and responding to everything else. We can see this responsivity everywhere. In an ordinary sense, plants respond to water and sunlight. Bodies respond to the quality of food offered to them. Circumstances in our lives respond to our degree of skill in navigating them. Some of us can respond to the communications we receive from our subtle bodies and subtle energy.

Responsivity is the natural state of manifest life. When we are being driven by karmic habit patterns, responsivity turns into reactivity. Reactivity is when we act out of compulsion or habit in a less than fully aware way. When we do sadhana, we rediscover more reciprocity and responsivity. Responsivity is both awake and playful. You clearly see and sense your circumstance and you respond to it appropriately and skillfully. Reactivity is always clumsy, out of step, out of tune, and ill-timed.

Despite our experience of suffering, more awake beings and reality as a whole are enjoying dualistic experience. When our senses and inner eyes open, we can directly sense the gladness in the experience of meeting that is inherent in more subtle manifestations of reality, such as the primordial lights of the five elements. The five elements—earth, water, fire, air, and space—comprise all appearings in the manifest world. But they have more subtle forms as colored lights that can be seen by people whose senses are more open. An exquisite responsiveness and exuberant gladness in meeting is apparent at this level. When we perceive it, we instantly feel that same joy.

Philosophers and spiritual traditions have long talked about cause and effect. But cause and effect is a very gross and mechanical description of the living process that is our actual circumstance in duality. The responsivity of the supreme subjectivity to itself as it plays in duality can more properly be understood as a pervasive phenomenon of call and response. As we wake up, we become increasingly sensitive to the call-and-response nature of manifest life.

For instance, from a mechanical View, you might say that the cause of hearing a sound is your ear. But from the View of Trika, the experience of physical ears has arisen in direct responsivity to the primordial capacity for sounding. The appearance of a physical ear is actually a response to the call of sound. The ear is meeting sound. The nose appears to meet smells with smelling. The eyes appear to meet sights with seeing. If you cook a beautiful meal for friends, tongues are meeting tastes with their capacity for tasting.

Furthermore, these arisings to meet are devotional. The total responsivity of the Supreme is an expression of primordial devotion, a devotional feeling that permeates all of reality. Whatever you do or don't do is being met just as the devotee runs to meet the beloved.

Call and response is built into many spiritual practices. Kirtan is a living symbol of the call-and-response nature of dualistic life. When we play kirtan, we get to practice being more spontaneous and devotional listeners and responders. The Tantras are also written in a call-and-response format with either Shiva or Shakti asking questions and the other responding. Satsang, an ancient form of gathering with a teacher, is a call-and-response practice. Puja is also call and response. You make offerings and are responded to with the return of your offerings as prasad, or a gift from the divine. These practices give us the opportunity to let go and participate in dualistic experience as ritual and the expression of primordial devotion.

31

Rest in your real nature

The essence of direct realization practice is to relax into uncontrived naturalness and spontaneity.

A teacher once said to me that the whole of the practice can be summarized in five words: rest in your real nature. We relax our self-concepts and karmas. We learn many kinds of sadhana to help us to do this. These practices require effort and discipline. But eventually we realize that the greatest austerity is to stop all struggle, to give up all objections and complaints, and yield to life just as it is.

Yielding is definitely not a condition of passivity; it is a condition of total receptivity and utterly spontaneous responsivity. We work with life's ever-changing circumstances in a graceful, skillful, practical, and positive way. We meet them just as we would a good friend. A good friend may be happy or sad, easy or difficult, but we care for our friend with the same tenderness and quality of attention nonetheless. Just so, we play with and adapt to circumstances as they are rather than willfully struggling to have our way and falling into anger and despair when life serves us difficulties.

Naturalness is the best word for what we discover and embody when we self-realize. Primordial naturalness, sahaja, is totally uncontrived and unconditioned by history, circumstance, linear time, conceptual space, or form. There is nothing missing. There is contentment with everything exactly as it is. The natural state is complete and replete.

Immersion in living presence introduces us to the eternal. We can begin to identify with permanence while still enjoying impermanence. Our sense of time radically changes, and the feeling of panicked urgency about our lives in samsara begins to recede. The fear of loss and death loses its grip on us. Many times people have the experience of a homecoming. It's a home and a heaven coming at the same time.

When you are resting naturally and at ease, there is simply no more urgency or mission or compulsion. You recognize everything, including your limitations, as an ornament of the natural state. You can be light and playful even in the face of your own "failings" or illness or loss. All sense of worry dissipates even as you have tremendous power to act.

Struggle is replaced by receptivity, practicality, devotion, and humor. You are going along with life in partnership, in friendliness, and with a laugh. You are a player in a cosmic play with no rehearsal and no script. You enjoy the full palette of emotions, yet nothing sticks or bogs down. It is all improvisation.

> In the natural condition, the space beyond limitations and partiality,
> Whatever presents itself, I enjoy as an ornament.
> So I don't make any effort to obtain or reject anything.
> — Chögyal Namkhai Norbu[18]

Even though we are generally not experiencing sahaja until we are more awake, we are also not unnatural even in our relative condition of limitation. Limitation is an experience created by the unlimited for its own enjoyment. So we are not trying to fix ourselves. The attitude that we are damaged, or evil, or trying to fix ourselves is diametrically opposed to this tradition. There is nothing here that is not a perfect expression of the essence nature, so there never is anything wrong. By engaging in sadhana, you are simply God playing at letting go of some natural Self-imposed experiences of limitation.

At the same time, "letting go of limitation" requires effort. It takes intelligence and creativity and effort to stop struggling. If we want to re-integrate our body, energy, and mind with living awareness, we will have to work hard for some time.

Luckily for us, sadhana is also a natural Self-imposed expression. There is beauty to it, but no ultimate significance. We are accomplishing our nature by making the effort to do sadhana. That's all. It is very simple.

32

Ananda is aesthetic appreciation

Lord Shiva eternally contemplates his own nature in a state of wonder and amazement at the Self.

The Sanskrit word used to describe the state of natural contemplation is *ananda*. Ananda means something like "bliss-clarity." There is no accurate English equivalent. The ananda of the Lord is not some kind of gross experience of a tingly, happy body. It is fathomless aesthetic appreciation: utter delight in experiencing and contemplating the creative nature of the Self.

We participate in the natural state of self-contemplation in our own, more limited way. The feeling you have when you finish making a work of art, writing a poem, or a piece of music, or cooking a beautiful dish, is an echo of ananda. You have a feeling of contentment and appreciation. You feel wonder at the simple fact that you made something. It is almost a surprise. You can't get over it. You want to keep contemplating and enjoying your own nature through what you have created.

You have externalized a self-expression and enjoy the recognition of what you have made out of yourself, but there is also an aspect of discovery. It's like unexpectedly coming across a sparkling gem and yet knowing it to be your self. In Vajrayana traditions this feeling is called "vajra pride." Vajra pride indicates the indestructible confidence that you begin to feel because you have experienced your real nature. It is not small-self prideful. In fact, vajra pride is the most innocent, and I would even say humble expression, because you are in a state of continual surprise at your own nature.

Ananda also includes a kind of clarity that is hard to imagine if we have not experienced it for ourselves. Entering the primordial state of contemplation is accompanied by the advent of blazing clarity in one's vision, mind, and other senses. If a person zoomed in an instant from the ordinary sensing they are experiencing right now to a condition of experiencing the clarity of ananda, they might find it very difficult to tolerate. The clarity of insight into the condition of beings and circumstances, along with the saturation of colors, sharpness of shapes, and the quality of light would be too piercing and intense. As our awareness and senses become more integrated with the natural state, this clarity can extend to other times and places, and even past lives. Luckily, as we do sadhana, our body, energy, and mind recalibrate over time and prepare us for this opening into clarity. Ananda, this cosmic bliss, is more like wonder or amazement at the freshness, beauty, diversity, and intelligence of everything.

33

Everything is equality

Everything is made by and of wisdom. The only difference between one circumstance or being and another is the degree to which enlightened essence nature stands revealed or concealed.

Eka means "one." *Rasa* means "taste" or "flavor." Eka rasa is also sometimes referred to as *samarasa* – "same taste." Our real situation is that there are infinitely diverse phenomena enjoying absolute equality. All are equally composed of wisdom virtue. All are self-expressions of one continuous enlightened subjectivity. When someone is established in this recognition and embodies it in their attitudes and behaviors, they are said to be in a condition of eka rasa.

Rasa also means "nectar" and carries the connotation of something that is nourishing and sweet. A person who is *rasika* possesses an appreciation for art and aesthetics. When one is established in the recognition that everything is equality, a deep aesthetic appreciation for manifest life and the perception of the sweetness and goodness of the creation naturally arise. Realizing the equality of all phenomena is one way of defining self-realization.

We encounter many different circumstances in our lives. We have strong feelings and convictions about whether circumstances are good or bad, just or unjust, traumatic or pleasurable, or desirable or undesirable. For instance, a person may hold a strong conviction that eating meat is sinful and harmful. If they see animals being killed for food, or if they should somehow be forced to eat meat, they will suffer. They may even be traumatized. Another person holds the conviction that eating meat is healthy, normal, and necessary. If they should be prevented from eating meat for some time, they may feel upset and suffer from that. These responses are conditioned.

Even our responses to the most extreme circumstances are conditioned. Nearly everyone on earth would agree that being thrown into a prison camp, starved, and tortured is bad. Yet some Tibetan monks and Lamas report that they were grateful for that circumstance because it helped them to deepen their realization. Every reaction that we have based on good or bad, just or unjust, traumatic or pleasurable, or desirable or undesirable is conditioned by karmic vision. No one particular reaction to a circumstance is necessary or the same for all people.

If you are in an art museum or gallery, you will see many paintings. When you see a painting of a war with people being hurt, you may feel emotions looking at the painting. The emotions you feel, or thoughts that arise, while looking at works of art are an aspect of self-contemplation. You are contemplating the human condition, your own condition, or the process of art-making. You know paintings are made of paint. You can be moved by a painting, but you do not have the same reactivity to them as you would if you saw the depicted situation in real life.

In terms of the View, a painting of a war and an actual war are both aspects of creative, alive wisdom: the Self expressing itself. On one level, they are unique and different expressions, but on another level, they are all "painted" by and within the natural state.

Neither a painting of a war or an actual war enjoys substantiality in the way we normally assume. Neither circumstance involves an objectively existing object (a painting) or beings (people). Both the painting and the actual war are real experiences, but as in a dream, both are being projected from and within a single subjectivity. The experience of externality, of objectivity, and of others is the creative life process of one continuous awareness and its energy.

When you can feel and see this for yourself, your level of reactivity and suffering goes down. You begin to have a deep appreciation for the wisdom and goodness and beauty and fecundity of the manifest world. You become more of a rasika. As Anandamayi Ma put it: "Even in the midst of this Lila [the play of the manifest], Oneness remains unimpaired. What is enjoyed in Lila is rasa, which is unique."[19]

Someone who is in the condition of eka rasa does not stop feeling compassion and other emotions. This is a mistake people often make when talking about eka rasa. They think it means that you wander around with a neutral affect, feeling nothing because everything is "equal." How boring! No one would do years and lifetimes of spiritual practice if this were the ultimate result! No one would follow a teacher who displayed no compassion or other emotions.

Human emotions are colors on God's palette, or flavors on God's tongue. They are meant to be savored. When we recognize eka rasa, that all is the Lord, we experience emotions in a more enlightened way. We instantly recognize the wisdom inherent in our emotions and all circumstances. With that recognition, we simultaneously embody and express wisdoms such as compassion more fully, not less. Our expressions of wisdom virtues are just less conditioned and more universalized. They leap toward others gladly and spontaneously like clear rainbow light continually flashing forth from the source.

34

Ethics are already built in

The natural state is goodness itself with no opposite. "Bad" is a play of *that*.

Generally, ethics is defined as a system that identifies right and wrong and gives us rules for acting according to what is deemed right. Punishment for wrongs may also be included.

Some systems of ethics lean more toward holding right and wrong as absolute values given either by nature, birthright, or God. Other systems of ethics tend to be more or less contextual, taking into account times, cultures, and actors. One thing that all systems of ethics have in common is the View that human beings have ethical shortcomings.

The fundamental understanding of Trika Shaivism is that there is only goodness, there is only beneficence. When we reintegrate with the natural state, we rediscover primordial goodness, and we understand directly that what we considered to be "bad" or "limited" or "flawed" is a self-expression or play of wisdom.

> *These two cycles, bondage and liberation, are the play of Lord Śiva and nothing else. They are not separate from Lord Śiva because*

differentiated states have not risen at all. In reality, nothing has happened to Lord Śiva.

— Abhinavagupta[20]

The absolute View of all direct realization traditions is "everything is fine." This insight into the nature of reality has been expressed in many, many ways by different teachers. The 16th Karmapa, former leader of the Kagyu tradition of Tibet, reportedly made this reassuring statement on his deathbed in an attempt to provide solace to a grieving student: "Nothing happens."[21]

Reality is and remains fine despite the insane variety of manifest life and the relative experience of suffering. Nothing happens other than that diverse projections of a continuous awareness and its energy arise and subside. When you realize that everything is happening within and is made of one continuous Self, you understand there is no question of ethics; there is no right and wrong because there is, in absolute terms, no other. There is no one to be harmed or benefitted. There are no objects, worlds, or beings in the ordinary sense. Right and wrong are relative experiences. They are real experiences, but at the base one discovers only goodness and its play.

And yet we are individuated styles of Shiva nature subject to the relative experience of separateness. We are subject to limited experiences of space and time. These real experiences, and the paradigms we concoct to navigate dualistic karmic vision, are also part of the play. God is immanent in the experience of limitation and the unlimited natural state.

Direct realization traditions are not transcendental. We are not ignoring manifest life or using absolute View to escape dealing with our real feelings and experiences of diversity. Where is there to escape from or to?

If we are not going to escape, and we are not going to be fully realized any time soon, what should we do? What should we not do? These are questions with which we need help!

Our traditions generally offer us precepts to live by. Precepts are a kind of ethical system, but instead of being grounded in "right" and "wrong," they are grounded in a View of how to functionally manage our bodies, energy, and minds in order to create the best circumstances for self-realization.

For instance, "Be actually honest" is a precept for my students. If you are thinking in a more ordinary way, you might say that honesty is good or right. But from the perspective of View, honesty supports the immune system and contributes greatly to one's ability to persevere and roll with life's ups and downs. Honesty also keeps one out of a lot of unnecessary karmic entanglement and demonstrates basic respect for others which simplifies life and helps to conserve everyone's vital energy. Honesty is an important aspect of *ahimsa*, nonviolence.

From a functional perspective, what we should do is what helps us to conserve energy; unwind karma; and relax our body, energy, and mind. What we should not do is anything that gets us more entangled in limitation and tension. The precepts of direct realization traditions are resources students can use to specifically enact this functional View until they are more realized and can naturally and spontaneously feel for themselves how to move toward waking up while living in a messy world.

An aspect of modern spiritual ethics that needs to be considered is the common instruction to cultivate compassion or cultivate kindness or generosity. In direct realization traditions, if we are being true to the View, we are not thinking or practicing in this way.

Compassion, kindness, and generosity are already built into the fabric of reality. These wisdom virtues are present in full measure everywhere even though it may not seem so from our limited perspectives. The sun of natural virtue is shining fully in all times and circumstances. It would not make sense to say "I am cultivating sunlight." The remedy is not to try to generate or cultivate anything, but to destroy the clouds of ignorance that obscure wisdom virtues from manifesting fully through us.

The most ethical thing we can do is practice and realize. We can try to be resting in natural presence as much as possible. The least ethical thing we can do is to stop trying to do that. To whatever extent we have reintegrated with primordial presence, that is the extent to which natural wisdom virtues will appear in us in their more expansive expressions.

Ethics is already "built in." So if you want to do good, do your practice and discover your indestructible goodness. Until then, you can act skillfully by following precepts and functionally managing your energy and interactions with others.

35

The heart is the gateway to unconditioned wisdom

Immersing yourself in the cave of the heart, you discover all guidance, all understanding, all virtue, all space, and the supreme moment.

Trika sadhana strongly focuses on the heart chakra or the heart space, *hridayakasha*. Accompanying this emphasis is the primacy of devotion in the teachings and writings of the tradition. In the Trika, these are front and center from the start.

What is the heart?

The heart is the seat of wisdom. Immersion in the heart space through meditation and mantra is a royal road to the encounter with unconditioned wisdom virtue.

Abhinavagupta writes:

> *When by virtue of the store of the gems of supreme wisdom, which are collected in the treasure house of the mystic heart, the state of Mahesvara (the Great Lord) is reached, one realises "I am all; what misfortune can befall, and to whom?"*[22]

The heart is also the subtle form of Kashi, the City of Light. The geographical Kashi (Varanasi, Benares) is one of the oldest, continuously inhabited cities in the world. It is the earthly mytho-poetic home of Lord Shiva in his householder form. The city also *is* Lord Shiva. Our heart space is Shiva's home in us. Here he resides in the "courtyard of duality,"[23] content and at rest in the midst of life as *jivanmukta*, one who is liberated in life.

Shiva as the renunciate yogi lives in the Himalayas. In the human subtle body, Shiva's Himalayan home is the seat atop the crown, just above sahasrara chakra. After the ascent to the Himalayas, there is always a return to the heart, to Kashi.

The heart is also the mahasandhi, the great juncture or portal between the manifest and the unmanifest, between linear time and Great Time. We explore our individualized sandhi of the heart, but in truth, the heart is at the center of reality, filling all space. The creation emerges continuously from this heart.

Finally, the heart is 'A', the first letter of the Sanskrit alphabet. This sound form, when used in sadhana, evokes the unconditioned, *anuttara*, the Lord. 'A' is the all-pervading, spontaneous freedom, *svatantrya*, that sits behind and is the summation of all sound forms including the unstruck sounds of the heart chakra. It is propelled by 'HA', Shakti. With her breath, with the power of the word, she excites the emission of the creation. 'A' is immanent in the destination 'MA': the last sound form in the Sanskrit alphabet and a living symbol of the manifest world. These three together, unconditioned awareness, the force, and their unity in the manifest world continuously sound the mantra AHAM, the "I am" of the totality.

36

Devotion is wisdom's crucible

Devotion arises simultaneously with the dawning of self-knowledge and hosts every action of awakened devotees.

It doesn't matter where you begin in spiritual life. You may be a skeptic. You may be a rationalist. You may be a *bhakta* (devotional worshipper). Wherever you begin, if you travel all the way back to discover your real nature, you will end in devotion. Contacting wisdom is contacting devotion. Knowledge of the Self is the getting of devotion. Just as with the famous heat and light of a flame, wisdom and devotion may be talked about separately, but they always arrive together.

Alive, aware presence appears as the physical world. It also appears as energy: the fundamental vitality and clarity of everything. When we travel to the center, it reveals itself to be wisdom, but not wisdom in the ordinary sense of knowing. The wisdom revealed, what composes all and of which all is composed, is wisdom virtue: goodness without an opposite, compassion, generosity, a profound intelligence beyond imagining, playfulness, gladness, clarity, and delight.

When we are immersed in the fullness of our own self, the Self, we overflow with these virtues naturally. We are good because of goodness. We are compassionate because of compassion. We are intelligent because of intelligence. There is no external circumstance that selectively calls forth these virtues; they continually pour out without restraint or reason.

A crucible is an alchemical vessel for making offerings and receiving blessings of wisdom. Devotion gathers and concentrates all wisdom virtues into itself and ignites them in a cosmic puja, a cosmic play of the ritual offering of self-to-self.

Dreams of mastery and the spiritual mountaintop are karmic fantasies of the less-than-realized. This mad devotion of Self to Self, born of wonder and amazement at its Self, makes the awake ones eternal servants of the Lord. To be a disciple is to be still on the path. To become like Shiva, a devotee of all, is the destination of all disciples.

> *I am only a servant and there is no master to be seen. This is a wonder to me.*
> — Utpaladeva[24]

37

The View expires

The ultimate instruction, beyond which there is no need for instruction, is *hold no View*.

In the key Trika text, the *Vijñana Bhairava Tantra*, Shakti asks Shiva for clarification of a variety of complex View teachings. At the end of her extensive list of questions, Lord Shiva replies:

> All this is nothing but a phantom for frightening children, or a sweet given by the mother (to attract the child). These descriptions are only meant for the spiritual advancement of the unenlightened.[25]

Since nearly all of us are unenlightened, Lord Shiva goes on to address Shakti Devi's questions and to offer 117 practical methods for "children." But the message is clear: the View teachings that are for so long our ground must eventually become the cliff that we jump from.

The Trika tradition is so far from dogmatism that it builds in its own obsolescence. Knowing this is wonderful for students. You can use the View. You should even become attached to View. But if you follow the practice through to its conclusion, you will not get stuck with anything other than the intimacy and immediacy of immersion in primordial livingness, your own Self.

We have many tools and words to get us there. We have our teachers. But once we have remembered, once we have relaxed the boundaries of body, energy, and mind, we don't need the View anymore. The View becomes the direct experience we are always living in, and whatever that is cannot be held by the View.

Swami Lakshmanjoo describes the letting go of the intricacies of View and, in essence, all of the accoutrements of spiritual tradition, as a bitter medicine.[26] But it is only bitter when we are attached to limited knowing and the security of believing that we have "gotten it" and that "it" is of supreme importance.

Nature unfolds and refolds itself with both utter simplicity and dazzling variety. Our destiny is to relax, immersed in presence while enjoying our reclaimed ability to play freely in the field of infinite arisings. Eventually, we can happily reconcile ourselves to the fact that all View teachings, even absolute teachings, come with an expiration date.

Keep on continuing

During a trip to India, I met a young Bengali man who worked at the Anandamayi Ma ashram on the banks of the Ganga in Varanasi. His parents were devotees of Ma, and he had grown up in her presence.

During the course of the visit, he told me about a cassette tape he had recorded of Ma giving satsang. He promised to translate it for me. Some months later, I received this. These words have inscribed themselves in my mind and heart and guide me always.

> *You have come for Darshan, but you still remember your home and family members. You have come for Darshan, you have come to the place where the Lord lives (vaikunt), where there is no knot (kunt). Here, you should try to have satsang. You should try to have Satbhava, Satvachan, and the stories told here should be about Reality without limitation.*
>
> *You do Masters Degrees. You do research and write books. But THIS knowledge is not in books... it is in you. That is the real knowledge, the real wisdom. On the path of sadhana,*

of satsang, you gain Atma Shakti, Atma Prakasha. You gain introduction to your real self. You tread on the path to Self-realization. The effort should not be stopped. Keep continuing. Become a pilgrim to openness, to awakening. Keep on continuing. It will happen. Let there be coming and going. The Thing will be done.
— Anandamayi Ma

Endnotes

1. Constantina Rhodes Bailly, *Shaiva Devotional Songs of Kashmir: A Translation and Study of Utpaladeva's Shivastotravali* (State University of New York Press, 1987), 84.
2. Quoted in Thomas McEvilley, *The Shape of Ancient Thought: Comparative Studies in Greek and Indian Philosophies* (Kindle Locations 1890-1893). Allworth Press. Kindle Edition.
3. Quoted in Ksemaraja, *Pratyabhijñahrdayam: The Secret of Self-Recognition*, trans. Jaideva Singh (Delhi: Motilal Banarsidass, 1982), 33.
4. Abhinavagupta, *Gitartha Samgraha, Abhinavagupta's Commentary on the Bhagavad Gita*, trans. Boris Marjanovic (Varanasi: Indica Books, 2002), 27.
5. Wikipedia contributors, "Hakuin Ekaku," Wikipedia, The Free Encyclopedia, https://en.wikipedia.org/w/index.php?title=Hakuin_Ekaku&oldid=825382096 (accessed April 24, 2018).
6. B. P. Bahirat, *The Amritanubhava of Jnanadeva* (Bombay: Popular Prakashan, 1963), 85.
7. Quoted in John Hughes, *Self Realization in Kashmir Shaivism: The Oral Teachings of Swami Lakshmanjoo* (Albany: State

University of New York Press, 1994), 21.
8. Anandamayi Ma, "Ma in Her Words," privately circulated PDF, multiple translators and sources, 149.
9. Anandamayi Ma, "Mataji's Amara Vani," *Ananda Varta*, Shree Shree Anandamayee Sangha, Varanasi, Vol. VI:2, 1958: 130.
10. Jyotish Chandra Roy, "Reduce Yourself to Zero," *Amrit Varta*, Shree Shree Anandamayee Sangha, Varanasi, Vol. IV:4, Oct. 2000: 22.
11. Swami Lakshmanjoo, *Shiva Sutras: The Supreme Awakening*, (Culver City: Universal Shaiva Fellowship, 2007), 156.
12. Swami Lakshmanjoo, *Light on Tantra in Kashmir Shaivism: Chapter One of Abhinavagupta's Tantraloka* (Kindle Locations 6944-6945). Universal Shaiva Fellowship. Kindle Edition.
13. These texts are Somananda's *Shivadrishti*, Utpaladeva's *Ishvarapatyabhijñakarika*, Abhinavagupta's *Isvara-Pratyabhijña-Vimarsini*, and Kshemaraja's *Pratyabhijñahrdayam*.
14. Raffaele Torella, *The Īśvarapratyabhijñākārikā of Utpaladeva with the Author's Vrtti*, (Delhi: Motilal Banarsidass, 2013), 86.
15. Torella, 87. The word in Sanskrit that Utpaladeva uses for "certainty" is *abhijñana*: remembrance or recognition.
16. Anandamayi Ma, "Matri Vani," *Ananda Varta* 27, no. 2 (1980): 87-88.
17. Coleman Barks. *The Essential Rumi: New Expanded Edition* (Kindle Location 1938). HarperCollins. Kindle Edition.
18. Chögyal Namkhai Norbu, *The Little Song of Do as You Please*, trans. Enrico Dell'Angelo (Arcidosso, Italy: Shang Shung Publications, 2017), 23.
19. Anandamayi Ma, *Words of Sri Anandamayi Ma*, trans. Atmananda (Haridwar: Shree Shree Anandamayee Sangha Kankhal, 2008), 145-146.
20. Hughes, 32.
21. *The Lion's Roar*, directed by Mark Elliot (1985; Colorado, Crestone Films) DVD.

22. Abhinavagupta, *Paramārthasāra of Abhinavagupta: Essence of the Supreme Truth*, trans. Deba Brata SenSharma (New Delhi: Mukatbodha Indological Research Institute, 2007), 122.
23. Jñanadeva, 85.
24. Swami Lakshmanjoo, *Hymns to Shiva: Songs of Devotion in Kashmir Shaivism; Utpaladeva's Shivastotravali* (Lakshmanjoo Academy Book Series) (p. 251). Universal Shaiva Fellowship. Kindle Edition.
25. Swami Lakshmanjoo, *Vijnana Bhairava Tantra: The Practice of Centring Awareness*, trans. Bettina Bäumer (Varanasi: Indica, 2002), 12.
26. Ibid., 12.

Acknowledgments

Unending gratitude to all those teachers and other beings who have taught me the View and who continue to push and prod me so I don't get stuck. Many thanks to my students Matridarshana Lamb and Ambika Beber for shouldering the load of running Jaya Kula Press and helping to share the teachings. Special thanks to my designer, Saskia Nicol, for somehow getting it and translating the View into color and form. Thanks to all of my students who continue to show up on the cushion and everywhere else. You make the impossible possible.

About Jaya Kula Press

Jaya Kula Press is a project of Jaya Kula, a registered 501(c)3 nonprofit organization headquartered in Portland, Maine.

Jaya Kula Press supports dharma practitioners by presenting spiritual teachings that are precise, practical, faithful to their origins, and yet accessible to a wide range of people. We currently publish the teachings of Shambhavi Sarasvati, the spiritual director of Jaya Kula.

About Jaya Kula

Jaya Kula is a vibrant, nonprofit householder community offering opportunities to learn and practice in the direct realization traditions of Trika Shaivism and Dzogchen. Visit jayakula.org for more information and Shambhavi's teaching schedule.

Made in the USA
San Bernardino, CA
17 November 2018